WHAT PEOPLE ARE SAYING ...

Contentment is no one's default condition. Like the apostle Paul, we all need to "learn" to be content, and this book will help you do just that. Within these pages, the idea of living a contented life is directly connected to better relationships with your family, neighbors, and coworkers. Pastor Jeff Gipe clearly points out that the key to all of these relationships is our communion with Christ. Read this book and begin your own quest for contentment!

Andy Deane
Director, Calvary Chapel Bible College
Murrieta, California

It is easy to be discontented in life. For some, this is the stimulus which leads them to Jesus. Yet, even Christians experience seasons of discontentment. In *Contented*, Pastor Jeff willingly shares some of his own battles in this area. During the course of these struggles, he discovered that "the key to the contented life is communion with Christ." It is my prayer that through this book, many will discover and experience this life-changing truth.

John Pennell
Pastor, Calvary Chapel of Lake Villa
Lake Villa, Illinois

No coincidence crossing paths with Jeff Gipe. Just God.

Years ago, I was launching a weekly Bible study at my company when I bumped into an old friend. Jeff was developing a series based on the apostle Paul's encouraging, but challenging words, "... for I have learned in whatever state I am, to be *content*" (Philippians 4:11 NKVJ).

What a privilege to be a part of that first group as Jeff slowly and carefully unpacked the apostle's teachings from Philippians 4. Before long, twenty of us were meeting weekly—two-thirds of my staff at the time! For many of the difficult lessons, Jeff drew from his own powerful testimony. This topic resonated loudly and clearly, and every single person benefited. Even those who didn't attend were impacted by the Spirit-led changes in their coworkers.

We are primed for a "Contentment" refresher and truly excited to read Jeff's study in book form!

Tristan Zafra
President & CEO, Trisoft Graphics Inc.
Costa Mesa, California

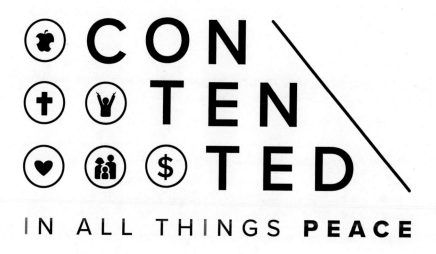

CON TEN TED

IN ALL THINGS **PEACE**

JEFF E. GIPE

CONTENTS

FOREWORD

Our culture lauds success! Winning isn't everything—it is the only thing! We live in a country where opportunity abounds, where risk-taking is rewarded, and where the American dream is idolized.

But what happens when we cross the finish line, when we achieve our goals but still find ourselves empty on the inside? What do we do when we discover that the richness of life that success promised us, and that we trusted in, was merely an illusion, a hologram without substance?

Over the past thirty years, Jeff and I have been business partners, partners in ministry, and close friends. I have watched the hand of God lead Jeff on his own search for contentment.

In this deeply honest and transparent book, Pastor Jeff Gipe recounts his own pursuit of success and examines the truths God showed him along the way. He discovered that what his soul longed for was not success, as defined by the world, but contentment. And the secret to contentment is communion with Christ in every area and season of life.

Regardless of the season you are in, *Contented* invites you to examine what you are pursuing and to question its ability to deliver on its promises.

What you chase will determine where you end up, and in this timely book, you will be challenged to consider how your life could be different if you pursue communion with Christ as your goal.

John Knapp
Pastor, Calvary Chapel Green Valley
Henderson, Nevada

ACKNOWLEDGMENTS

> Just as our bodies have many parts and each part has a special function, so it is with Christ's body. We are many parts of one body, and we all belong to each other. In his grace, God has given us different gifts for doing certain things well.
>
> *Romans 12:4–6a*

Jesus, in His grace, brought many people alongside me with different gifts to do this book well. I owe a debt of gratitude to Mary Pero, Lindsay Gipe, and Romy Godding for making *Contented* better than I could have ever done on my own.

To my son, Tyler, I am so grateful for all of your support and keen artistic eye.

To my longtime friend, John Pennell, thank you for your pastoral support and input.

To my good friends, Dean Yorimitsu and Ashley Garcia, thank you for the web page and amazing book cover designs!

To my NCL church family, thank you for inspiring and encouraging me through the process, especially you who were so gracious to allow me to share your testimonies.

Special thanks to Teresa, my wife of forty years, who has been by my side through thick and thin. You have always been and continue to be a great source of encouragement to me, especially on those days when I was discontent writing a book about contentment in all things. I love you!

But most importantly, I am grateful to my Lord and Savior, Jesus Christ, who lovingly allowed me to experience His love and grace in ways that revealed to me, without a doubt, the key to the contented life is communion with Christ.

INTRODUCTION

At age nineteen, I read Dale Carnegie's book, *How to Win Friends and Influence People.*[1] This book affected me so greatly, I enrolled in the training seminars, "The Secrets of Success." I immediately began applying these principles to my life, and ten years later, I had reached a comfortable level of affluence.

I owned my own company, made six figures, owned my own home, and drove a nice car. I was married to my lovely wife, and we had a wonderful son. I seemed to have everything a person could want or need, yet somewhere deep inside, I felt something was missing. I wasn't satisfied.

On April 14, 1990, my family and I were flying back from a vacation in Mexico. I wasn't feeling well that morning from being out drinking the night before. As the turbulence tossed me back and forth and turned my stomach upside down, a gnawing sense of something missing grew into an overwhelming feeling of desolation. I was a thirty-year-old successful man with everything going for me, yet I was empty.

The Pursuit of Happiness

Can you relate? Are you satisfied with your life? Have the things you've acquired made you happy? Or is there a gnawing sense of emptiness inside? In 2016, I stumbled across an article in *Bethesda Magazine* titled, "The Reasons of Our Discontent." The opening lines caught my attention: "Bethesda-area residents are among the best-educated, highest paid, healthiest people in the nation. So why are people complaining they're not happy? A look at existential angst."[2]

What was true for me appears to be true for many. The quest for happiness is one people have been on for a long time. The article went on to ask, "We're all searching for happiness, aren't we? But what does it take to be truly happy?"[3]

Within the article, the writer explored several of the biggest pursuits of happiness: money, health, and education. I had all of that and still felt something was missing. So did the people of Bethesda. According to a 2012 report in *Money Magazine*, the Bethesda area boasts one of the highest median family income rates in the nation. *Forbes* recently named Bethesda the most educated small town in America, as more than half its residents have a graduate or professional degree. In 2012, the American College of Sports Medicine ranked Greater D.C. the second fittest area in the United States.[4] The residents of Bethesda appear to have it all.

Dr. Robert Hedaya, a thirty-four-year resident of Bethesda, as well as the founder of the National Center for Whole Psychiatry in Chevy Chase, Maryland, and a clinical professor of psychiatry at the Georgetown University School of Medicine, estimates that fifty percent of the people living in the Bethesda area are "mildly to severely unhappy" with a "growing sense of unhappiness and lack of fulfillment. … It doesn't really matter how much you have," he says, "because there's a sense that it's never really enough. A lot of people are asking, 'Is this all there is? Is this it?' Like a drug, the benefits of power and money are transient, and one always needs another fix. Until a person can step out of this paradigm, happiness will remain elusive."[5]

What is driving this discontentment?

The Root of the Problem

On that flight home from Mexico with my wife and son, something hit me. Dale Carnegie's seminars had certainly delivered on the promised results. I had become successful following his principles. But success was not the secret to happiness, fulfillment, or contentment, and I hadn't even realized that I was hoping it was. Something else was still missing.

As that reality struck, I turned to my wife and said, "This Sunday is Easter. Do you want to go to church?" I don't know who was more shocked by my question. We had not stepped foot into a church together since our wedding day twelve years earlier. We went that Easter Sunday and agreed to go one Sunday a month.

A few months later, something took place in my heart that still astounds me to this day. The Gulf War was in full swing, and the pastor started to teach about prophecy. I was sitting in a pew surrounded by two thousand people, but I felt like he was staring right at me as he read this passage:

> You should know this ... that in the last days there will be very difficult times. For people will love only themselves and their money. They will be boastful and proud, scoffing at God, disobedient to their parents, and ungrateful. They will consider nothing sacred. They will be unloving and unforgiving; they will slander others and have no self-control. They will be cruel and hate what is good. They will betray their friends, be reckless, be puffed up with pride, and love pleasure rather than God.

> *2 Timothy 3:1–4*

That was me. These words described precisely who I had become. I had spent my entire life being influenced by self-help books seeking to learn the secrets of success in the pursuit of health, happiness, wealth, and education. But all I had found was emptiness. The root of the problem was not *too much* success, wealth, health, or education. The root of the problem was sin. The people the pastor read about loved themselves more than God, and so did I. Soon after that, I accepted Jesus as my Lord and Savior.

At age thirty-one, the gnawing sense of emptiness was finally gone. I felt complete. Content.

The Quest for Contentment

Years after my Sunday morning experience with God and my subsequent conversion, I was sitting at a conference listening to a young pastor share from God's Word. It was June 2015. At this point, I had been pastoring a church for ten years. As I listened to this young man share, I realized that even as a pastor, there were still areas in my life where I was not truly content. I wanted things in my fellowship to be different. I wanted God to do the same things in my church that He was doing in other churches.

As I wrestled in my heart with these things, I came across a passage written by the apostle Paul:

> Not that I was ever in need, for I have learned how to be content with whatever I have. I know how to live on almost nothing or with everything. I have learned the secret of living in every situation, whether it is with a full stomach or empty, with plenty or little. For I can do everything through Christ, who gives me strength … At the moment I have all I need—and more!
>
> *Philippians 4:11–13, 18a*

"At the moment I have all I need—and more." These words hit me hard. This passage perfectly described what I was looking for. And everyone else is looking for the same thing, whether they realize it or not. I wanted to know more about the contented life Paul spoke of, so I launched deeper into that quest.

Thus began my pursuit of God and for the contented life found only in Him.

The word *contented* is defined by *Merriam Webster* as "feeling or showing satisfaction with one's possessions, status, or situation." For this book, I have chosen to use the word *contented* rather than *happy*, as happiness is most often associated with a feeling, whereas contentment is more of a state of being or a state of mind. God seems more concerned with contentment than happiness, as Scriptures like this reveal: "Yet true godliness with contentment is itself great wealth" (1 Timothy 6:6).

God knows the value of contentment and desires His children to experience it.

Are you in pursuit of the contented life? Have you felt a sense of dread and guilt that even with all you have, there must be more? I invite you to look to God with me for answers on our quest for the contented life.

Whether you have never set foot in a church or have been going for years, I believe you will find the answers you are looking for in this book. In the pages that follow, we will explore:

- The Cause of the Discontented Life
- The Cure for the Discontented Life
- The Conduct of the Contented Life
- The Culmination of the Contented Life

Do you want more? Are you looking to strengthen the connection in your relationships with your spouse, your children, or your friends? Would you like to find a deeper satisfaction and sense of fulfillment in your workplace or with your colleagues? Are you looking for a greater purpose?

Join me as we begin this journey together. I'm so glad you're here.

THE **CAUSE** OF THE DISCONTENTED LIFE

"YOU SAY, 'THAT IS STRANGE: IF I HAD A LITTLE MORE I SHOULD BE VERY WELL SATISFIED.' YOU MAKE A MISTAKE: IF YOU ARE NOT CONTENT WITH WHAT YOU HAVE YOU WOULD NOT BE SATISFIED IF IT WERE DOUBLED."[6]

C. H. SPURGEON

Has this ever happened to you? One day, you finally attain the very thing you thought would make you happy, but it doesn't? Your business is finally successful, but now you *need* to expand. You've worked hard on your marriage and improved it, but the relationship isn't as fulfilling as you hoped it would be.

Sonja Lyubomirsky, a professor of psychology at the University of California, Riverside, and author of the book, *The How of Happiness*, was also quoted in the *Bethesda* article. She said, "Studies of twins suggest that genetic factors account for 35 percent to 50 percent of a person's propensity for happiness."[7] According to Lyubomirsky, as much as half of our capacity for happiness is genetically determined by "our biological mother or father or both, a baseline or potential for happiness to which we are bound to return even after major setbacks or triumphs."[8]

At first, I thought Lyubomirsky's suggestion sounded unfair. *Some people have good genetics and are content while others have bad genetics and are discontent?* As I considered it more, however, I realized she may be on to something. Even with my Christian beliefs of God being in full control, I don't entirely disagree with her findings. Genetics may play a role in our state of contentment, or lack thereof. But whenever there is discontent, the root cause is always sin.

THE GARDEN

> Then the LORD God formed the man from the dust
> of the ground. He breathed the breath of life into the
> man's nostrils, and the man became a living person.
> Then the LORD God planted a garden in Eden in the
> east, and there he placed the man he had made.
>
> *Genesis 2:7–8*

The book of Genesis talks about the garden of Eden, a real place where the first created man and woman, Adam and Eve, lived in harmony with God and their surroundings. It was perfection. The garden provided all they needed in terms of food and shelter, and their relationship with God and one another provided all they needed in terms of emotional, physical, and spiritual satisfaction.

This is what we are all looking for in our search for contentment. It was unique and creative and deeply meaningful to be a part of God's creation. Adam's work must have been immensely satisfying, as he had been *created* specifically for the task. Every animal God made was brought to him to be named. His wife, Eve, was created from him and for him. While she had her own unique purpose and design, she was also the perfect complement to Adam in every way.

Adam had fulfilling work, a flourishing relationship with his wife, and a God he knew intimately. The Bible says God Himself walked with Adam and Eve in the cool of the garden each day. Adam knew who he was and was sure of his purpose, and he had the best companion to share it all with. Adam and Eve were living in a perfect world.

So what went wrong?

THE CHOICE

> The LORD God placed the man in the Garden of Eden to tend and watch over it. But the LORD God warned him, "You may freely eat the fruit of every tree in the garden—except the tree of the knowledge of good and evil. If you eat its fruit, you are sure to die."
>
> *Genesis 2:15–17*

Within the garden of Eden, God planted the Tree of the Knowledge of Good and Evil. This was the one tree within the garden from which they were not permitted to eat. This restriction was their *only* rule. But God made it clear—the consequence of eating the fruit of this tree would be costly:

> If you eat its fruit, you are sure to die.

But Adam and Eve both ate its fruit.

> The serpent was the shrewdest of all the wild animals the LORD God had made. One day he asked the woman, "Did God really say you must not eat the fruit from any of the trees in the garden?"
>
> "Of course we may eat fruit from the trees in the garden," the woman replied. "It's only the fruit from the tree in the middle of the garden that we are not allowed to eat. God said, 'You must not eat it or even touch it; if you do, you will die.'"
>
> "You won't die!" the serpent replied to the woman. "God knows that your eyes will be opened as soon as you eat it, and you will be like God, knowing both good and evil." The woman was convinced. She saw that the tree was beautiful and its fruit looked delicious, and she wanted the wisdom it would give her. So she took some of the fruit and

ate it. Then she gave some to her husband, who was with her, and he ate it too. At that moment their eyes were opened, and they suddenly felt shame at their nakedness. So they sewed fig leaves together to cover themselves. When the cool evening breezes were blowing, the man and his wife heard the LORD God walking about in the garden. So they hid from the LORD God among the trees.

Genesis 3:1–8

Sin had entered the world. The word *sin* is an old English archery term that simply means "to miss the mark." Adam and Eve had sinned, and their choice would have costly consequences.

Even within the perfect living conditions of work, home, and family, Adam and Eve were still tempted. They still sinned. And they are the ideal representation of mankind since we all would have done the same thing. The apostle Paul referenced this event much later in the book of 2 Corinthians, saying Eve was actually deceived by the serpent. She bought the lie that she was missing out on something.

Herein, we see the ultimate cause of our discontent.

It is not simply the act of sin (biting into the fruit), but believing the lie.

Either:

God is withholding something from us.

Or:

We know better than God what is good and right for our lives.

Eve believed the fruit would give her something good, so she ate. But she was deceived. What Eve did not know was that her choice to eat this fruit, though it gave her the knowledge she had hoped for, would also bring death to herself and her husband, as well as future generations. Did they die immediately? No, they did not. But it was a life-altering, *spiritual death* in an instant. Their connection with God and each other was never the same.

But why did God give mankind the freedom to choose? If He is all-knowing, or omniscient, then why would He put a tree in the garden of Eden knowing Adam and Eve would partake, thus allowing sin to enter the human race? This question has been asked for centuries. I believe the simplest answer is because God loves mankind with an everlasting love and created mankind out of this love. He wanted to give mankind the choice to love Him back. True love is always based on choice. So, God put a "choice tree" in the garden, as if to say, *I will leave this tree as a choice for man, to choose Me and My love for him, or not. My love for him will remain, but I will never force him to love Me back.*

THE COST OF SIN

> When the cool evening breezes were blowing, the man and his wife heard the LORD God walking about in the garden. So they hid from the LORD God among the trees. Then the LORD God called to man, "Where are you?"
>
> He replied, "I heard you walking in the garden, so I hid. I was afraid because I was naked."
>
> "Who told you that you were naked?" the LORD God asked. "Have you eaten from the tree whose fruit I commanded you not to eat?"
>
> *Genesis 3:8–11*

God made it clear: forsaking communion with Him was a costly choice. "If you eat its fruit, you are sure to die." His warning is undoubtedly that of spiritual death. When we choose to do what God has told us not to do, we cut ourselves off from communion with Him. This also entails physical death, since God is the source of both physical and spiritual life. The moment Adam and Eve chose to disobey God, the human body began to decay. The process of physical death in the body begins slowly. Each day our bodies are on earth, they grow older and closer to death. The spiritual death of Adam and Eve, however, was immediate.

The genetic condition of sin had entered the world. All future generations of the human race would be infected with this genetic disorder and suffer the consequences, the primary effect being separation from God. The result of their sin was not, as some might think, a *punishment* from God for their actions. It was a *consequence*. There was an immediate disconnect in their relationship with God, their Creator and Life Giver. This is what sin always does. It separates us from God and from each other. It tears relationships apart and causes us to care only about ourselves.

Shame

Did you notice this? When the Lord called to Adam and Eve in the garden, they hid themselves. Genesis 3:8–11 says they hid because they were afraid. What were they afraid of? Quite simply, they were guilty. They didn't *feel* guilty. But they were, and this brought the feeling of shame. Standing in front of a Holy God in their nakedness and sin caused this feeling and the attempt to hide. Not surprisingly, Dr. Mary C. Lamia, Ph.D., calls shame a dangerous emotion:

As a self-conscious emotion, shame informs us of an internal state of inadequacy, unworthiness, dishonor, regret, or disconnection. Shame is a clear signal that our positive feelings have been interrupted. Another person or a circumstance can trigger shame in us, but so can a failure to meet our own ideals or standards. Given that shame can lead us to feel as though our whole self is flawed, bad, or subject to exclusion, it motivates us to hide or to do something to save face. So it is no wonder that shame avoidance can lead to withdrawal or to addictions that attempt to mask its impact.[8]

Dr. Brené Brown, a social worker and researcher of shame and vulnerability, writes this on the subject:

Based on my research and the research of other shame researchers, I believe that there is a profound difference between shame and guilt. I believe that guilt is adaptive and helpful—it's holding something we've done or failed to do up against our values and feeling psychological discomfort.

I define shame as the intensely painful feeling or experience of believing that we are flawed and therefore unworthy of love and belonging—something we've experienced, done, or failed to do makes us unworthy of connection.

I don't believe shame is helpful or productive. In fact, I think shame is much more likely to be the source of destructive, hurtful behavior than the solution or cure. I think the fear of disconnection can make us dangerous.[9]

Shame causes us to try to hide from God and from one another. Rather than drawing us closer into fellowship and communion, it draws us apart into isolation. It is a powerful tool used by Satan when we fall short of God's righteous standard.

The consequences of sin are costly: shame, separation, and a disconnection from God's original purpose and design. Where once God looked at His creation and saw goodness, now it was marred by sin. Wholeness and openness were now replaced by brokenness and shame; intimacy and closeness now exchanged with separation and disconnection.

Loss of His Image and Likeness

A tragic consequence of the first sin was the loss of God's image and likeness upon mankind.

> Then God said, "Let us make man in our image, after our likeness."
>
> *Genesis 1:26a ESV*

There are a few ways we are made in God's image. The most obvious refers to our spiritual nature. Man was created with body, soul (spirit), and mind—a trinity forming one person—just as God Himself is also a Trinity—Father, Son, and Spirit—yet still one God.

In addition to man being created in God's image, man is also created in God's likeness. This refers to the abilities man is given or the things man is called to do. One example is creativity. God infused into man the ability to create, just as God, the ultimate Creator, created everything. In this way we are like Him. God also gave mankind a unique ability to communicate and connect with Him and with one another. By the words of God's mouth, He spoke the entire creation into existence. By the words of God's mouth, He spoke blessings on

His creation, His most beloved mankind. By the words of the mouth of man, he has been given the ability to bless and praise his God and fellow man. Being made in God's likeness should produce such results.

There was once the ability to create more beauty to glorify God; we now find man using these abilities to hurt their fellow man. Where once man had the ability to create works of art that drew men's eyes to God, man now praises and receives praise for himself. Man uses the gift of communication to curse and tear down rather than to bless. Man uses the ability he has been given for intimacy as an opportunity to gain power and oppress the weak. James, the brother of Jesus, spoke about this issue:

> People can tame all kinds of animals, birds, reptiles, and fish, but no one can tame the tongue. It is restless and evil, full of deadly poison. Sometimes it praises our Lord and Father, and sometimes it curses those who have been made in the image of God. And so blessing and cursing come pouring out of the same mouth. Surely, my brothers and sisters, this is not right!
>
> *James 3:7–10*

Loss of Fellowship

The most costly consequence of sin was man's separation from God. Genesis 3:8a implies God had a habit of daily walking with Adam and Eve in the afternoon, or during the "cool of the day." This suggests a certain intimacy, fellowship, or friendship between mankind and God. Another word for this fellowship is "communion," or *koinonia* in the Greek. Koinonia, among other things, means fellowship, community, and communion.

The word *fellowship* is used often in the Bible. The *Tyndale Bible Dictionary* defines it as "communion with God, which results in common participation with other believers in the Spirit of God and God's blessing." We were made for connection and fellowship, but communion, this intimate relationship with God, was lost due to sin.

This loss also affected man's personal relationships with his wife, his children, and even his workplace. In Genesis, we see God instructing Adam about his relationship with work:

> And let them have dominion over the fish of the sea and over the birds of the heavens and over the livestock and over all the earth and over every creeping thing that creeps on the earth.
>
> *Genesis 1:26b ESV*

God also instructed him in his relationships with his wife and future children:

> Then God blessed them and said, "Be fruitful and multiply."
>
> *Genesis 1:28a*

Genesis 3 reveals more results of the curse following Adam's sin:

> Then he said to the woman, "I will sharpen the pain of your pregnancy, and in pain you will give birth. And you will desire to control your husband, but he will rule over you." And to the man he said, "Since you listened to your wife and ate from the tree whose fruit I commanded you not to eat, the ground is cursed because of you. All your life you will struggle to scratch a living from it. It will grow thorns and

thistles for you, though you will eat of its grains. By the sweat of your brow will you have food to eat until you return to the ground from which you were made. For you were made from dust, and to dust you will return."

Genesis 3:16–19

Creation, Adam's workplace, would now produce thorns and thistles. More effort and labor would be required. For Eve, her pregnancies and deliveries would no longer be an entirely joyous occasion. Childbearing would now be marked by pain. We accept these things as reality now, but can you imagine birth without pain and work without sweat? How wondrous were God's intentions for man?!

Notice the change in dynamic between Adam and Eve's relationship. Where once they were commissioned to govern and rule over the earth together, now Adam would have to scrape by to make a living. Work would be his focus and be more difficult because of the fall. Much more time would be needed with very poor returns. Eve would also suffer from this curse. Her unique ability to help Adam would now be changed into the need to control him. And why not? He's working all day and not getting much done!

Man was created for communion:

- Communion with God, his Creator and the Author of his purpose.
- Communion with his spouse, his helpmate and lover.
- Communion with his children and fellow man.

All of these benefits were lost in the fall, the result of man's sin.

The sad truth is these connections are broken and lost each and every day. As previously stated, sin begins when we believe that God is withholding something from us, or somehow we think we know better than God what is good and right for us. When we seek to have authority over ourselves rather than seeking God's purpose for us, we will inevitably find a trail of broken relationships leading to a wasteland.

We were created for communion with God and for fellowship with our fellow man. Constant communion with God, walking each day in the cool of the garden, as Adam did, fulfills the deepest need in us to know who we are and why we are here. Who else can answer that question but God? When we break this communion through sin, we lose connection to the One who knows us most intimately. This loss of connection results in a lack of direction, a lack of identity, and a lack of understanding of what our relationships with others should look like.

The loss of communion with God immediately affects our fellowship with our fellow man—our spouse, our children, our colleagues, or our neighbors. It makes everything and everyone out of order. Without communion with God, we fight to prove our value, our sense of self-worth, and our purpose on this earth. We aren't sure if God or our loved ones are withholding things from us. We aren't sure if they really do have our best interests at heart.

Without God, we are all wandering through some level of discontent, whether at home with our families or at work with our fellow man. This is the result of sin passed down from generation to generation, tracing back to Adam and Eve in the garden. We are still living with the consequences and the curse of sin.

The reality of sin and the state of mankind answers so many questions as to why the world is the way it is today. Sickness, wars, terrorism, shootings, and horrible crimes are all a result of living in a fallen world. There are people who like to think they are above sin, or untainted by its effects. They go about doing their good works, contributing to social justice movements, and trying their best to make positive changes in the world. These are good things and valiant efforts. But the Bible teaches that no one is good (Romans 3:10–12). Whether we like it or not, we have all been affected by the curse of sin. We aren't sinners because we sin. We sin because we are sinners. Jesus brought this truth even closer to home when He said:

> You have heard that our ancestors were told, "You must not murder. If you commit murder, you are subject to judgment." But I say, if you are even angry with someone, you are subject to judgment! You have heard the commandment that says, "You must not commit adultery." But I say, anyone who even looks at a woman with lust has already committed adultery with her in his heart.
>
> *Matthew 5:21–22a, 27–28*

The truth of sin is a heavy weight to bear. Knowing we prove our sinfulness and contribute to this fallen world every day can leave us feeling hopeless or spur us to go on a journey toward finding a cure. We inherited a fallen nature, and we are discontent. If no one is good and we can't produce good on our own, is there a cure to be found?

THE
CURE FOR THE
DISCONTENTED LIFE

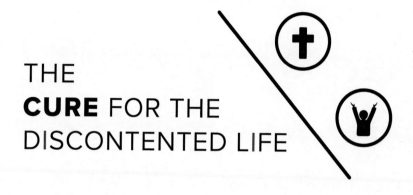

"THE KEY TO THE CONTENTED LIFE IS COMMUNION
WITH CHRIST."

JEFF GIPE

B efore becoming a Christian, my business was successful. I attained said success by methods that were not always ethical, admittedly. My conversion in February of 1991 had not made my life easier, nor had it made my problems—problems I had created for myself—go away. In March of 1992, some of my past choices were catching up to me. Rather than own up and suffer the consequences, I decided to run away from it all and purchased a property in Big Bear, California.

Big Bear is a quaint, charming mountain community not very far from where we were living in Orange County. My wife and I would often go there with our son to enjoy the snow during the winter and the lake during the summer. Relocating there seemed like the perfect solution to my problems. I would get away from it all. My wife and I bought some property and had plans drawn up for our dream home. I imagined sitting on the front porch looking out into the wilderness and listening to the wind whistle through the pine trees. This was my picture of peace.

On June 28, 1992, a large earthquake hit Big Bear, causing all kinds of problems for us. Our contractor was so busy fixing and repairing damaged homes, he didn't have time to work on ours. Meanwhile, our home in Orange County fell out of escrow, not once but twice. We couldn't sell our current home and couldn't build our new property. We were stuck. My peace was replaced by panic.

In the midst of my fear, I called my pastor and invited him to lunch. I had met Pastor Carl Westerlund on a trip to Israel six months earlier. He was the director of the School of Ministry at Calvary Chapel Costa Mesa. As I sat across the table from him, my anxiety over the state of my life kept me from even touching my lunch. Then I began to spill my guts. "Carl, why would God allow all of these things to happen to me?"

"Jeff," he replied, "peace is not found in a place, it is found in a Person. When that Person rules and reigns in your life, *then* you have peace."

I had tried to run away from my problems. I had been looking for contentment by changing my surroundings. But true contentment will not change with your surroundings, your circumstances, or by the attainment of your future goals. True contentment is found only when communion with God is restored.

The only cure for our discontent, for our fallen state, is communion with Christ. Communion with Christ is the key to the contented life we all seek.

The Christian life is referred to as a journey, or a walk of faith. And attaining contentment comes not through a formula or a set of procedures, but as we experience daily, ongoing communion with Christ. And therein lies one of the great paradoxes of the Bible: communion with Christ is something you receive both instantaneously, when you accept Jesus as your Lord and Savior, and over the course of your life, as you grow in the grace and knowledge of Him. Your first true experience of contentment occurs when you realize your need for heaven and for Him, but that will not be enough to carry you through the rest of your life.

Salvation is merely the foundation to begin your journey to the contented life. It all begins when you make peace with God.

A PEACEFUL LIFE

> Jesus said, "Peace I leave with you, My peace I give to you; not as the world gives do I give to you. Let not your heart be troubled, neither let it be afraid."
>
> *John 14:27 NKJV*

What was lost in the garden of Eden when Adam and Eve sinned? It was so much more than exile from the perfect surroundings and the ideal life God had created for them. It was much more costly than Adam and Eve first realized. The genetic condition of sin had entered the world. All future generations of the human race would be infected with this disorder and suffer the consequences, the worst being separation from God Himself. When Adam and Eve sinned, they were immediately sent out from God's presence. This may seem harsh, but a Holy God cannot commune with sinful man. This does not mean God forsook them, or that His heart did not yearn for them. The book of Genesis tells story after story of a Holy God pursuing and calling His people back to Him.

> Then the LORD called to man, "Where are you?"
>
> He replied, "I heard you walking in the garden, so I hid. I was afraid because I was naked."
>
> "Who told you that you were naked?" the LORD God asked. "Have you eaten from the tree whose fruit I commanded you not to eat?"
>
> *Genesis 3:9–11*

When my oldest granddaughter was a toddler, one of our favorite games to play at the park was hide-and-seek. As soon as we would arrive, she'd say, "You count ten, I hide." Then she'd run and hide behind a tree. She never checked to see if

I was watching but focused only on running and finding her spot. Of course, being a loving and protective grandfather, I would watch her every move and see exactly where she went. After counting to ten, I'd call out, "Where's Penny?" And again, "Where's Penny? Is she hiding behind the water fountain? Is she hiding behind the sign? Is she hiding behind the slide?" As I called out her name, I'd walk toward the tree and hear her giggling. She'd jump out from behind the tree before I could say her name again, laughing hysterically. We would do this over and over and over again.

This is a similar picture of what happens when we try to run and hide from God. We may think He can't see, but He loves us too much to ever take His eyes off of us. I love how God called out to His two kids, Adam and Eve, saying, "Where are you?" He knew exactly where they were. And He knows where we are too. He knows what we have done, and He allows us to come undone, the first step to freedom from the trap of sin.

Imagine what Adam and Eve must have felt. What pain they must have endured as a consequence of their sin. They suffered the death of Abel, their beloved son, at the hands of Cain, his brother, because of jealousy and anger. How they must have ached, knowing the origin of this act. How they must have grieved, seeing the effects of sin on the world around them. The repercussions infected everything, even creation itself.

Like Adam and Eve, I have often tried to hide from the consequences of my sin. I have tried to find peace elsewhere outside of God. Like Adam and Eve, I have discovered there is no peace or contentment there.

The beauty of the gospel is found in this simple truth:

> For this is how God loved the world: He gave his one
> and only Son, so that everyone who believes in him

will not perish but have eternal life. God sent his Son into the world not to judge the world, but to save the world through him.

John 3:16–17

God knew that outside of Him, our search for contentment would be in vain. So He sent His only Son, Jesus, to die upon the cross of Calvary. The blood of Jesus was the price required for our sins. This act of selfless, unconditional love, in spite of our choices, in spite of our sin, shows the true heart of God. And He is still calling out for us, still yearning to walk and commune with us in the cool of the garden. Speaking of this great act of love—Jesus dying for our sins—Paul said:

> Yes, Adam's one sin brings condemnation for everyone, but Christ's one act of righteousness brings a right relationship with God and new life for everyone.
>
> *Romans 5:18*

The apostle Peter wrote:

> Christ suffered for our sins once for all time. He never sinned, but he died for sinners to bring you safely home to God. He suffered physical death, but he was raised to life in the Spirit.
>
> *1 Peter 3:18*

Only through Jesus can we be saved and restored. The price our sin required was the blood of Jesus, which He willingly gave. By receiving this gracious gift of forgiveness, we can be restored into communion with God once again. Communion with God is the cure for our discontentment.

Communion with Christ begins when we make peace with God. By acknowledging and accepting the sacrifice of His Son, Jesus, we receive the free gift of salvation offered to all.

Paul said this:

> Therefore, since we have been made right in God's sight by faith, we have peace with God because of what Jesus Christ our Lord has done for us. Because of our faith, Christ has brought us into this place of undeserved privilege where we now stand, and we confidently and joyfully look forward to sharing God's glory. We can rejoice, too, when we run into problems and trial, for we know that they help us develop endurance. And endurance develops strength of character, and character strengthens our confident hope of salvation. And this will not lead to disappointment. For we know how dearly God loves us, because he has given us the Holy Spirit to fill our hearts with his love.
>
> *Romans 5:1–5*

Making peace with God will lead us to the peace that only God can give. This is not a peace the world promises, but the peace that Jesus promises. It can only be experienced in His presence, "this place of undeserved privilege where we now stand." This must have been a radical statement to the reader of that day, when the Jew was separated from God's presence by a curtain in the temple and the Gentile was separated by the wall around the temple. But when Jesus died, "the curtain in the sanctuary of the Temple was torn down the middle" (Luke 23:45), and "he broke down the wall of hostility that separated us" (Ephesians 2:14). Jesus' work on the cross gave every Jew and every Gentile access to His presence, and that access applies to us today.

One of the greatest privileges to those who have made peace with God is that, "when we run into problems and trials," we will find the peace of God. It is natural for us to run from our problems and trials. But when you run into His presence in the trying times, then you will experience the supernatural peace of God.

The word for *trials* literally means "pressure." And pressure, as you know, is the process used to turn coal into diamonds. In the same way, God uses pressure in the life of His children to transform us into the image of Christ.

Paul knew all about this:

> We are pressed on every side by troubles, but we are not crushed. We are perplexed, but not driven to despair. We are hunted down, but never abandoned by God. We get knocked down, but we are not destroyed. Through suffering, our bodies continue to share in the death of Jesus so that the life of Jesus may also be seen in our bodies.
>
> *2 Corinthians 4:8–10*

Paul saw the truth of life's pressures: since God is most magnified in them, they can and will produce joy within us:

> That's why I take pleasure in my weaknesses, and in the insults, hardships, persecutions, and troubles that I suffer for Christ. For when I am weak, then I am strong.
>
> *2 Corinthians 12:10*

Would you like to come to the place in life where you take pleasure in pressure? It begins when you stop running from your problems and run in to the presence of God, where you experience the Holy Spirit filling your heart with God's love.

The word in the Greek that describes God's love is *agapē*. It is a powerful and transforming word from which we get our

English word "agony." A brief survey of the Scriptures portrays this love as selfless, always giving to others:

> For this is how God loved the world: He gave his one and only Son, so that everyone who believes in him will not perish but have eternal life.
>
> *John 3:16*

> But the Holy Spirit produces this kind of fruit in our lives: love, joy, peace, patience, kindness, goodness, faithfulness, gentleness, and self control.
>
> *Galatians 5:22*

> Love is patient and kind. Love is not jealous or boastful or proud or rude. It does not demand its own way. It is not irritable, and it keeps no record of being wronged. It does not rejoice about injustice but rejoices whenever the truth wins out. Love never gives up, never loses faith, is always hopeful, and endures through every circumstance.
>
> *1 Corinthians 13:4–7*

What must we do to experience supernatural peace in every circumstance? Pastor, teacher, and author, Dr. M. G. Gutzke, gives the answer:

> True peace comes from yielding all to the will of God. Let him have his way, let him solve the problem, then the heart can be at peace. This is the peace Jesus had as he faced the agony of Calvary. It is peace grounded in the promise of the "joy set before him" (Hebrews 12:2). This is the peace offered to us. Christians do not need pleasures, affluence, influence, gratification or desires. Instead, they obtain peace through

fellowship with God. Their peace is within, and the world cannot understand it, nor can it take that peace away.[10]

The key to the contented life is found in fellowship with God. This fellowship can only be experienced when we run in to His presence with praise.

What is praise?

A PRAISE-FILLED LIFE

> We would worry less if we praised more. Thanksgiving is the enemy of discontent and dissatisfaction.[11]
>
> *Harry Ironside*

The apostle Paul's life was not an easy one. He was imprisoned, beaten, stoned, shipwrecked, bitten by a poisonous snake, wrongly accused, and much more. There must have been plenty of times he asked the question *why*.

Why would God allow trials and tribulations to happen to someone who loves Him? Many great men of the Bible have asked the same question. Job asked, "Why have You set me as Your target?" (Job 7:20 NKJV). David asked, "LORD, why do You cast off my soul? Why do You hide Your face from me?" (Psalm 88:14 NKJV). Jeremiah asked, "Why is my pain perpetual and my wounds incurable?" (Jeremiah 15:18 NKJV).

Paul remained mesmerized by the marvelous mercies of God. He considered all God had done for him and how everything good comes from God, and it moved him to a place of praise in spite of his circumstances.

> For God has imprisoned everyone in disobedience so he could have mercy on everyone. Oh, how great

are God's riches and wisdom and knowledge! How impossible it is for us to understand his decisions and his ways! For who can know the LORD's thoughts? Who knows enough to give him advice? And who has given him so much that he needs to pay it back? For everything comes from him and exists by his power and is intended for his glory. All glory to him forever! Amen.

Romans 11:32–36

This is real praise. It is a joyful assessment of all that God has done for you, in spite of your present circumstances. Another word for praise is thankfulness. The Bible is filled with examples of praise to God in the form of dancing, singing, and shouting, with and without musical instruments. The saying, "Praise the Lord," is found nearly 250 times in the Bible, as people touched by God's mercy and goodness thank Him for what He has done, in both good times and in bad.

Praise and thankfulness will carry us through the harder seasons in life, those times when we are prone to ask, "Why, Lord?" When we praise God, we remember and reflect upon what He has done for us. This act alone enables us to frame our present circumstances, no matter what they may be, within God's understanding. God sacrificed His only Son on the cross on our behalf so that we could receive forgiveness and eternal life. We can trust that He has our best interests in mind. We can trust that He is in control and knows what He is doing.

In the gospel of Luke, there is a story about ten lepers, which exemplifies our need to praise God in every circumstance.

As he entered a village there, ten men with leprosy stood at a distance crying out, "Jesus, Master, have mercy on us!" He looked at them and said, "Go show yourselves to the priests." And as they went, they were cleansed of their leprosy. One of them, when he saw that he was healed, came back to Jesus, shouting, "Praise God!" He fell to the ground at Jesus' feet, thanking him for what he had done. This man was a Samaritan. Jesus asked, "Didn't I heal ten men? Where are the other nine? Has no one returned to give glory to God except this foreigner?" And Jesus said to the man, "Stand up and go. Your faith has healed you."

Luke 17:12–19

Ten men were healed, but only one man returned to praise God. Can you relate? The key point is not that nine men were ungrateful and one man was thankful. The key point is that one man remembered and reflected on what had happened to him. Only one man made the effort to acknowledge his Healer by returning and praising God. The other nine were merely thankful that their circumstances had changed.

Those ten men would each go on to experience other trials in life. Nine men would be waiting for their circumstances to change in order to find their happiness and contentment. But the one man who returned, the man who remembered, reflected, and praised, he would have a much different foundation for future trials. He believed there was One he could go to and depend upon. This man would have the hope of Jesus, whether or not his situations ever changed. This man would be content.

And we know that God causes everything to work together for the good of those who love God and are called according to his purpose for them.

Romans 8:28

45

This kind of praise empties the heart of self and blesses the heart of God. This is the kind of praise God desires. When we praise this way, we commune with God, and that leads us to do what we were created for.

A WORSHIPFUL LIFE

> Worship is the art of losing self in the adoration of another.[12]
>
> *Joseph Carroll*

True worship is more than an emotional experience. It is the Lord God being so present in your life that you give yourself entirely to Him. It is coming to a place where you worship Him when you are alone, at home, with others, and at work. True worship is a continuous state.

Praise is an act of thanksgiving, a response to the merciful, gracious, faithful, and loving ways of God, whereas worship is an act of living, a devotion to Him because of what He has done for you. Praise can be a part of worship, but worship goes beyond praise. Worship gets to the heart of who we are. To truly worship God, we must let go of self-worship and ideals. We must be willing to humble ourselves before God, surrendering every part of our lives to His control, adoring Him for who He is, not just for what He has done.

Worship is a lifestyle, not an occasional activity. Jesus gave these commands:

> You must worship the LORD your God and serve only him.
>
> *Luke 4:8*

> For God is Spirit, so those who worship him must worship in spirit and in truth.
>
> *John 4:24*

To understand true worship, we must identify what it is not. Worship of self and idols will appeal to our natural man, but it is not of God. It has no place in God's plan for our contentment. Where self-worship and idolatry exist, true worship of God cannot. And we are all worshipping something. Jesus said this:

> Wherever your treasure is, there the desires of your heart will also be.
>
> *Luke 12:34*

Take a moment to think about the things that occupy your thoughts and mind. Consider the things you give the majority of your time to, whether intentional or not. These are your idols. These are your treasures.

These can be anything "under the sun," as King Solomon said. He spent his whole life searching for the contented life. He sought scientism, hedonism, capitalism, religion, materialism, humanism, and more, but all he found was emptiness. It is possible to make idols out of all the things King Solomon explored, including relationships, wealth, knowledge, power, success, sex, and self-gratification.

As Paul took a joyful assessment of all God had done for him, in spite of his present circumstances, he found himself in such a deep place of worship that he wrote:

> And so, dear brothers and sisters, I plead with you to give your bodies to God *because of all he has done for you*. Let them be a living and holy sacrifice—the kind he will find acceptable. This is truly the way to worship him. Don't copy the behavior and customs of this world, but let God transform you into a new person by changing the way you think. Then you will

learn to know God's will for you, which is good and pleasing and perfect.

Romans 12:1–2, emphasis mine

As I shared earlier, I first began to experience true peace when I gave my life to Jesus and began following Him in February of 1991. This moment was life-changing, to say the least. While that peace immediately removed the consuming emptiness, I still had moments when discontentment returned. Contentment in these times did not seem like a state of being, but momentary. I was still grasping for something more.

Paul encouraged us in the book of Romans to not rest in our moment of salvation. We must continue our quest for contentment as we surrender our lives, even our bodies, to God. This may seem like a scary proposition. Hearing this for the first time (or even the tenth) creates fear; in offering our lives to God, He may do something we don't want Him to do. "I don't want to be a missionary!" "I don't want to work in orphanages!" These fears can keep us from fully trusting God's plan. Whatever He has for us is what's best, and He will supply all we need to fulfill His plan.

God created you for a purpose. There has never been another person on earth just like you. You were created, flaws and all, to be a picture to the rest of the world of God's amazing grace. God loved you enough to send His Son to die for you, even when you were stuck in sin (Romans 5:8). Let these truths set your mind at ease. Fulfilling God's plan and will for your life is the only way to have true joy. Believe, take heart, and surrender.

You may be wondering why Paul used the word *bodies* and not just the word *lives*. Paul clarified his reasoning in the book of 1 Corinthians:

Don't you realize that your body is the temple of the Holy Spirit, who lives in you and was given to you by God? You do not belong to yourself, for God bought you with a high price. So you must honor God with your body.

1 Corinthians 6:19–20

Our bodies are the temple of the Holy Spirit. As discussed in the first section on the cause, God created mankind in His image and likeness. This image and likeness was distorted when sin entered the world. Thankfully, when we make peace with God by receiving His Son Jesus as our Lord and Savior, God fills us with His Holy Spirit. While this does not change our physical nature, it restores our spirit, or our inner person, with God's image and likeness once again. We become God's vessels to bring glory to Him and to bless others.

How do we position ourselves to begin truly living the contented life? First, we make peace with God. Peace comes from accepting God's ready forgiveness, made possible through the death, burial, and resurrection of Jesus. Second, we surrender our lives to God's will and purpose, fully trusting His ways are best. Because God's initial design for every man was for continual communion with Him, discovering and surrendering to the calling God has placed on our lives become the launching pad to living and maintaining a life of contentment.

Before it appears in Romans 12, the word *transform* is used three times in the New Testament. Two of these instances are in both accounts of Jesus' transfiguration. Peter, James, and John followed Jesus up to a high mountain. What they saw next was incredible:

As the men watched, Jesus' appearance was transformed so that his face shone like the sun, and his clothes became as white as light.

Matthew 17:2

This majestic vision was followed by the awesome voice of God proclaiming Jesus as His Son, telling those on the mountain to hear and listen to Him. How amazing this must have been to witness!

The transfiguration of Jesus is an example of what happens to us when we are transformed by God. The person we once were is gone. Those who knew us before see a radical change. Our new self reflects Jesus, a person set apart from the world. We can't help but clash with our former surroundings. God changes us so we can be used greatly for Him, a glorious transformation indeed.

This transformation doesn't happen instantly. It is a process that starts with changes from the inside out. The changes God makes within us, in our hearts and in our souls, become visible outwardly. And the only way to meet the challenges of changing our carnal minds is constant communion with Christ.

Author and evangelist Oswald Chambers wrote this:

We have the idea that we can dedicate our gifts to God. However, you cannot dedicate what is not yours. There is actually only one thing you can dedicate to God, and that is your right to yourself. If you will give God your right to yourself, He will make a holy experiment out of you—and His experiments always succeed. The one true mark of a saint of God is the inner creativity that flows from being totally surrendered to Jesus Christ.[13]

When we have communion with Christ, He transforms us from the inside out. When these changes reflect outwardly, we become witnesses of the power of God, doing the things the Lord wants us to do. When we surrender our bodies and our minds to the Lord, He truly makes a holy experiment out of us; and what flows forth is a life that is in the image and likeness of Jesus Christ.

A HOLY LIFE

> The reason why many are still troubled, still seeking, still making little forward progress is because they haven't yet come to the end of themselves. We're still trying to give orders, and interfering with God's work within us.[14]
>
> *A. W. Tozer*

Holiness has largely been misunderstood in our culture. With phrases like "You're so holy" or "holier-than-thou," and the acknowledgment that God is holy, we have clouded what should be a relatively simple subject.

What does holy mean? Renowned Bible teacher, author, and speaker, Warren Wiersbe, defined it this way:

> Our English word holy comes from the Old English word *halig*, which means "to be healthy, to be whole." What health is to the body, holiness is to the inner person. We use the word "sanctification" to describe the process of growing to become more like Christ, and "holy" to describe the result of that process.[15]

The Hebrew word for holy is *qodesh* and means "apartness, set-apartness, separateness, sacredness." The dictionary defines it as "dedicated or consecrated to God for a religious purpose; sacred."[16]

The prophet Isaiah described a vision he had of heaven:

> I saw the LORD sitting on a lofty throne, and the train of his robe filled the Temple. Attending him were mighty seraphim, each having six wings. With two wings they covered their faces, with two they covered their feet, and with two they flew. They were calling out to each other, "Holy, holy, holy is the LORD of Heaven's Armies! The whole earth is filled with his glory!"
>
> *Isaiah 6:1b–3*

Isaiah not only saw the Lord seated on His throne, but he saw mighty winged angels, or seraphim, surrounding Him, crying out, "Holy, holy, holy!" Seeing this image caused Isaiah to immediately recognize his own sinful state. He went so far as to pronounce doom over his sinfulness, uncleanliness, and unworthiness.

This is what it means to say that God is holy. He is separate from us. He is without sin. He is above us. The psalmist, speaking of God's holiness, said,

> O God, your ways are holy. Is there any god as mighty as you?
>
> *Psalm 77:13*

> There is none holy like the LORD; there is none besides you; there is no rock like our God.
>
> *1 Samuel 2:2 ESV*

Why is God holy and set apart from us? Because He is perfect, complete, and in Him is no darkness at all. He is love and does not act on selfish motives or ambitions. He only does that which is right, true, and just.

Would it surprise you then to hear that we have also been called by God to be holy? If you were to ask that question today, most would likely respond that God has called man to be happy, not holy. Yes, God does want us to be happy, but He knows that a person can only be truly happy when they live holy lives. God never said, "Be happy as I am happy," but we find eight times in the Bible that God said, "Be holy, for I am holy." Peter wrote:

> So you must live as God's obedient children. Don't slip back into your old ways of living to satisfy your own desires. You didn't know any better then. But now you must be holy in everything you do, just as God who chose you is holy. For the Scriptures say, "You must be holy because I am holy."
>
> *1 Peter 1:14–16*

God has called us to be *holy as He is holy. Holy* simply means to be set apart. When speaking of man, the word holy may be better described as "set apart for God and His purposes." God is calling us to be set apart for His purposes, knowing that we will find peace and contentment when we live holy lives.

There are many Christians today who would rather look exactly like the rest of the world in the ways they parent, treat family, conduct their businesses, and live their lives. This is one of the key reasons they find themselves with that same gnawing sense of discontent I was experiencing myself. Christians need holiness to differentiate themselves from the world and be sure they are living out God's purpose.

There was a popular phrase years ago in the church that said, "Too much of the world to be happy in Jesus and too much of Jesus to be happy in the world." Sadly, this is the current state many find themselves in. They have personally accepted Jesus as their Lord and Savior and have received His free gift of salvation and the forgiveness for their sins. But they have not come to a place of choosing to live a life set apart for God. They find themselves stuck between wanting to be more like Jesus and wanting to live like the rest of the world. This type of thinking and living simply does not work. It inevitably leaves one dissatisfied in both camps. It saddens me to see Christians who copy the behavior and customs of this world. They follow every philosophy under the sun, as King Solomon said.

This same king, who was the healthiest, wealthiest, wisest man to ever walk the face of the earth, came to this conclusion at the end of his life:

> "Everything is meaningless," says the Teacher, "completely meaningless! What do people get for all their hard work under the sun?"
>
> *Ecclesiastes 1:2–3*

The word *meaningless* is also translated "emptiness." In other words, everything under the sun leaves you with a gnawing sense of emptiness.

There is a reason God has called you to live a set apart life, as He is set apart. He created you to live in communion with Him. It is only when we experience true communion with God that we find ourselves whole, complete, satisfied, and content. We will never experience true contentment apart from God. It's just not possible.

The New Testament gives much advice and wisdom on how to be holy and how to live the set-apart life God has called us to. How are we to conduct ourselves while on this quest for the contented life?

Live Carefully and Spiritually

> So be careful how you live. Don't live like fools, but like those who are wise. Make the most of every opportunity in these evil days. Don't act thoughtlessly, but understand what the Lord wants you to do. Don't be drunk with wine, because that will ruin your life. Instead, be filled with the Holy Spirit, singing psalms and hymns and spiritual songs among yourselves, and making music to the Lord in your hearts. And give thanks for everything to God the Father in the name of our Lord Jesus Christ.
>
> *Ephesians 5:15–20*

People try to find contentment in countless ways. But they are essentially just attempting to fill the void, the emptiness. Alcoholism, pornography, drugs, sex, money, power, and righting wrongs in society are just a few ways people self-medicate. But it won't work. While some of these things may temporarily bring happiness or peace, they will not bring true contentment. They will often cause more pain than pleasure.

This is why Paul warned us to be careful how we live (verse 15). There are a number of worldly things that look appealing in the short-term but lead to disappointment in the long-term. Remember, I assumed success would bring me happiness and contentment. It did for a short time but proved to be fleeting. The moment success left, happiness did too. The path to contentment is filled with careful, godly steps.

Paul also encouraged us to be filled with the Holy Spirit (verse 18). The previous section discussed how God fills us with His Holy Spirit, restoring His image and likeness back to our inner person, or spiritual man and woman. The verb *filled* means, "keep on being filled." This *filling* is continual. It's

55

an experience we should constantly enjoy, not just on special occasions.

To be filled with the Spirit means to be constantly controlled by the Spirit in our minds, emotions, and will.

Going back to Romans 12:1–2, this is why Paul encouraged us to offer our bodies to God as living and holy sacrifices. When we surrender our entire lives to God, He fills us with His Holy Spirit, restoring His image and likeness back to us. When we live filled with His Holy Spirit and set our lives apart for His good purposes, we become holy as He is holy. We must literally be filled with His Spirit and His holiness in order to live out and do the good works He has prepared for us to do (Ephesians 2:10).

Learning to walk carefully and spiritually is the only way to live a holy, Spirit-filled life. God's Word gives the instructions for how to walk carefully, and experiencing God's presence through prayer reveals how to live spiritually.

A HUMBLE LIFE

> Because of the privilege and authority God has given me, I give each of you this warning: Don't think you are better than you really are. Be honest in your evaluation of yourselves, measuring yourselves by the faith God has given us.
>
> *Romans 12:3*

In order to have communion with Christ, we must first examine ourselves. We can't receive God's gift of forgiveness through Christ without first acknowledging we are sinners who need forgiveness. Self-examination is a key component in our relationship with God and with everyone else.

This is why Paul exhorted us three times to look carefully at ourselves. We must not think too highly of ourselves, but instead be honest and realistic about who we really are, measuring ourselves by our God-given faith. This doesn't have to be a difficult process. Thinking about ourselves constantly is what comes naturally, after all.

Paul had a different purpose in mind. When he instructed us to think about ourselves, it was for the purpose of knowing God's will for our lives. It is spiritually healthy for us to look into the mirror of God's Word and examine our lives through His eyes.

Notice Paul does not encourage us to conduct our self-examination by comparing ourselves to others. He does not ask us to count up our good works, or include how we *feel* about ourselves. Paul said we must measure ourselves "by the faith that God has given us." How do we do this? Addressing the Romans, Paul said this:

> So faith comes from hearing, and hearing through the word of Christ.
>
> *Romans 10:17 ESV*

The way to accurately measure ourselves by the faith we've been given is to measure ourselves by God's Word. In our self-evaluations, the Bible will show us how to avoid being too harsh or too lax with ourselves. We must measure ourselves solely by God's Word, where the faith we've been given originated. Who God says we are is who we truly are.

It's easy to judge others by our own standards of living. If you're someone who manages your finances well, it's easy to be critical of those who aren't financially responsible. If you enjoy a healthy marriage or have well-behaved kids, it's easy to judge those who are struggling in those areas. That, my friend, is human nature. This way of thinking means we are judging one another based on our own standards, not God's.

The majority of people I counsel usually fall into two different groups. There are those who tend to be more self-righteous, leaning heavily on their own good works, judging *others* more harshly than they judge themselves. Then there are those who tend to be more self-degrading, judging *themselves* more harshly than others. When we examine ourselves by our self-imposed standards, or by how the world sees us, we will most likely be wrong. Becoming a Christian does not lend immunity from self-centeredness. Even people with the best intentions can be led by self. Examining ourselves based on the truth found in God's Word is the only guarantee for a healthy view of self and others.

God gave us the Bible to read, meditate on, and apply to our lives. If we use it this way, God will transform us into the image and likeness of His Son. Then He will be better able to use us for His purposes. This process may take some time depending on our obedience or disobedience. But God has promised to transform us when we diligently seek Him through His Word.

After all these years of reading the Bible, I am amazed at its ability to continually reveal who I am while at the same time transforming me into a more holy person. The more submissive I am to the Word of God, the more I understand His perfect will for my life.

None of us have arrived, but we are on our way. Paul encouraged the Corinthians in this:

> So all of us who have had that veil removed can see
> and reflect the glory of the Lord. And the Lord—who

is the Spirit—makes us more and more like him as we are changed into his glorious image.

2 Corinthians 3:18

Paul made it clear that he was a work in progress.

I don't mean to say that I have already achieved these things or reached perfection. But I press on to possess that perfection for which Christ Jesus first possessed me.

Philippians 3:12–13

The word *possessed* means "to influence or control." God wants to govern our lives not for our own benefit, but that we might govern the earth.

Pride and Humility in Self-Examination

In his book, *Mere Christianity*, C. S. Lewis calls attention to "The Great Sin" in chapter 8. Any guesses as to what that might be?

Unchastity, anger, greed, drunkenness, and all that, are mere flea bites in comparison: it was through Pride that the devil became the devil: Pride leads to every other vice: it is the complete anti-God state of mind.[17]

If anyone would like to acquire humility, they first have to realize they are proud:

If you think you are not conceited, it means that you are very conceited indeed.[18]

In contrast, Lewis described what a truly humble man thinks of:

He will not be thinking about humility: he will not be thinking about himself at all.[19]

Lewis's description of humility matches the description of Jesus:

Is there any encouragement from belonging to Christ? Any comfort from his love? Any fellowship together in the Spirit? Are your hearts tender and compassionate? Then make me truly happy by agreeing wholeheartedly with each other, loving one another, and working together with one mind and one purpose. Don't be selfish; don't try to impress others. Be humble, thinking of others as better than yourselves. Don't look out only for your own interests, but take an interest in others, too. You must have the same attitude that Christ Jesus had. Though he was God, he did not think of equality with God as something to cling to. Instead, he gave up his divine privileges; he took the humble position of a slave and was born as a human being. When he appeared in human form, he humbled himself in obedience to God and died a criminal's death on a cross. Therefore, God elevated him to the place of highest honor and gave him the name above all other names, that at the name of Jesus every knee should bow, in heaven and on earth and under the earth, and every tongue confess that Jesus Christ is Lord, to the glory of God the Father.

Philippians 2:1–11

Only when we are in a place of humility will we be able to see who God created us to be. This is why Paul warned us to be honest in our self-evaluations. Some translations of the Bible say to "think soberly," which means to be levelheaded and earnest in our thoughts. This is how our minds can experience change. If pride is what keeps us from godly growth, humility is the remedy.

When we evaluate ourselves by the mirror of God's Word, we are certain to sober up. God is not just asking us to *feel* these things, but to think about them. Consider what it means to be made in the image of God. Consider what it means to be Holy Spirit-powered.

Many people are paralyzed by their past sins. The shame has caused them to feel flawed and unworthy of love and belonging, unworthy of connection. Whenever I am hit with these thoughts, I combat them with the truth of God's grace:

> God saved you by his grace when you believed. And you can't take credit for this; it is a gift from God. Salvation is not a reward for good things we have done, so none of us can boast about it. For we are God's masterpiece. He has created us anew in Christ Jesus, so we can do the good things he planned for us long ago.
>
> *Ephesians 2:8–10*

I read an article about an artist named Jane Perkins. She takes what most people would consider useless junk or trash and transforms it into a masterpiece. She has created the Mona Lisa and other classic works of art using buttons and all kinds of bits and pieces found lying around the house. It's beauty for ashes personified. And it's unbelievable. Extraordinary.

More extraordinary is that the Creator of the heavens and the earth has done the same with you and me. He has taken all the junk and trash you've accumulated in your lifetime and turned you into a beautiful work of art. When you realize this gracious truth, you have begun your discovery of the contented life.

God is collecting the broken pieces of your life and molding you into His masterpiece that you might be a witness of God's grace to the world. The Holy Spirit is essential for a fruitful life and a far-reaching ministry. This is why Jesus told the disciples to wait for it:

> But you will receive power when the Holy Spirit comes upon you. And you will be my witnesses, telling people about me everywhere—in Jerusalem, throughout Judea, in Samaria, and to the ends of the earth.
>
> *Acts 1:8*

Giving your bodies and minds to God is to say this: *Lord, I am Your empty vessel. Fill me with Your Spirit so Your grace and love will be poured out of my life for the good of others. Make me Your servant.*

A SERVING LIFE

> Just as our bodies have many parts and each part has a special function, so it is with Christ's body. We are many parts of one body, and we all belong to each other. In his grace, God has given us different gifts for doing certain things well.
>
> *Romans 12:4–6a*

One of my favorite things about the church is that it is one of the only places where every single person has a place and belongs. Just like in a family, each person has something unique they bring to the table. Paul compares this aspect of the church to the human body—it is made of many differing parts but comes together to form one complete frame.

Picture that for a moment. Each and every part of your body serves a specific purpose. Your eyes, your toes, your elbows, your mouth, your neck, your legs, etc. Is it possible to live without certain parts of your body, or with broken parts? Definitely. There are countless examples of this. It is called a disability because it usually takes additional strength from another part of the body to overcome the missing function.

The same is true of the church. Each person has a place and a purpose. When the church comes together, each person bringing their unique talents and gifts, the church becomes the active body God intended it to be.

This illustrates and defines service in the church: Believers from every tongue, tribe, and nation coming together for the singular purpose of sharing God's heart with the world through the use of their individual and collective God-given talents and gifts.

Service in the church may be passing out bulletins, setting up chairs, volunteering in the children's ministry, participating on the worship team, serving in a leadership role, or teaching. It may also be taking your workplace skill or passion and using it for God's church at large. For example, someone in the church who uses their drive and resources to provide ways to purify water in third-world countries is blessing the body of Christ outside of the church. Being an active member of the body of Christ within the church should overflow to serving God's world at large.

Unfortunately, there are many people who choose not to serve in the church. They think the church is after their money or they've been burned by other Christians or they simply don't see the significance in serving. What they don't understand is they are robbing themselves and the church of the gifts, talents, insights, and passions God has uniquely created them to use. Choosing not to participate within the body of Christ, or within a church, is not a passive decision. It is to choose to withhold, or render defective, one part of the body of Christ, the part God intended that person to fill. In such situations, the body is now forced to work harder to overcome the deficit, or disability.

The Bible calls the church not just the body of Christ, but the bride of Christ. Collectively, the church, or believers all over the world, form one single body. According to Paul, we are being prepared for marriage to the Lamb of God:

> I promised you as a pure bride to one husband—Christ.
>
> *2 Corinthians 11:2b*

> As the Scriptures say, "A man leaves his father and mother and is joined to his wife, and the two are united into one." This is a great mystery, but it is an illustration of the way Christ and the church are one.
>
> *Ephesians 5:31–32*

> Let us be glad and rejoice, and let us give honor to him. For the time has come for the wedding feast of the Lamb, and his bride has prepared herself. She has been given the finest of pure white linen to wear. For the fine linen represents the good deeds of God's holy people.
>
> *Revelation 19:7–8*

Imagine a marriage where one person refuses to participate. Marriage is hard work, requiring commitment and cooperation from each person. Back in Genesis, Eve was created as a "helpmate" for Adam (Genesis 2:18). They were the perfect complement to one another, each created with differing gifts and talents to contribute to the relationship. Coming together this way made them a new creation, one effectively functioning for God's glory.

From the beginning, God designed both marriage and the church to be a unit that accomplishes what one can't do alone. A marriage needs two people working together to thrive. A church needs all the believers working together to thrive. In both relationships, this isn't always easy and doesn't always happen naturally. But it is always worth the effort.

Our natural human nature is to resist or push away people who challenge our beliefs, actions, or words. We don't like it. Even when it's our spouse who loves us and has our best interests at heart, we don't like it. It's easy to chalk up these interactions to the fault or ill will of the other person. But what if God wants to use those who challenge our long-held beliefs or actions to help deeply change us? What if God wants them to help draw us to a place we wouldn't be able to go on our own?

This is God's heart and intent for the church. It is a place where believers of differing backgrounds and passions gather to challenge and encourage one another. It is a place where believers share their gifts and talents and come alongside one another to help those inside and outside the church.

The giving of yourself to share your gifts with others is what I call *transformed service*. You are so thankful for all God had done in and for you that there is a burning desire to use everything you have to bless others.

Transformed service has innumerous forms. Using these God-given gifts may mean sharing your special talents, your vocational skills, your capacity to help financially, or simply lending your time and efforts. Transformed service can be used for your local church, your neighborhood, or globally for God's church at large. The church is the place you can discover and practice the gifts God has graciously and uniquely instilled in you. It is the place God will provide opportunities for you to share your gifts with other believers and see the outcome.

Do you have the gift of teaching? If you're not sure, the children's ministry or other groups within the church could be great places to test this out. Do you have a passion for prayer? As a pastor, I'm always grateful for those who love to stand in the gap. So step out in faith and see how God might use that gift of intercession for His kingdom.

Maybe you're a businessman, like I was, and you already recognize you have the gift of leadership. While this may be true, transformed service means learning how to use this gift with the guidance, power, and sensitivity of the Holy Spirit. And it is within the church that God will help you practice this.

Maybe you have no idea what your gifts and talents are. If that's the case, immerse yourself in fellowship with faithful believers who will encourage you and serve alongside you. As you do, you will discover who God has created you to be and what He would have you to do in His service. He has great plans and purposes specifically for you—that is a guarantee!

A GIVING LIFE

As a pastor and former businessman, I would like to address the topic of financial giving. The Bible speaks in the book of Genesis about believers tithing a tenth of our income (Genesis 14:19–20; Leviticus 27:30–3). This act of giving back to God is done sacrificially and out of gratitude for what He has done in your life. The Bible also speaks about offerings, or what are commonly called "love offerings," which are above and beyond your tithe gift (Deuteronomy 12:5–6). If you have experienced any amount of success in your business, you have likely been asked to give to all sorts of organizations in need of your financial donations. The fact is, God has called everyone to be generous, cheerful givers, because that is how He has been toward us.

You must each decide in your heart how much to give. And don't give reluctantly or in response to pressure. "For God loves a person who gives cheerfully."

2 Corinthians 9:7

The word for *cheerfully* is the Greek word *hilaros*, which means "hilarious, prompt, and willing." We are all called to be cheerful givers, but those with more means are often asked to give more, especially to organizations doing God's work across the globe. In such situations, it is easy to give financially and not spiritually. Those giving large sums may convince themselves they are participating in God's ministry, when they are primarily checking a box to make them feel better about themselves. God can use whatever we give, but if it doesn't come from a gracious, Spirit-led heart, the blessing is missed by the giver.

For a believer, money is simply a tool. The Bible says God is the owner and supplier of all we have, including our finances. We are simply stewards of the gifts He has given to us.

For all the animals of the forest are mine, and I own the cattle on a thousand hills.

Psalm 50:10

Whatever is good and perfect is a gift coming down to us from God our Father, who created all the lights in the heavens. He never changes or casts a shifting shadow.

James 1:17

Again, it will be like a man going on a journey, who called his servants and entrusted his wealth to them. To one he gave five bags of gold, to another two bags, and to another one bag, each according to his ability. Then he went on his journey.

Matthew 25:14–15 NIV

This transformed view of money and talents makes it clear that God is not asking us to merely write and send checks on His behalf. He is asking us to participate in the work He is doing all over the world, sharing His love for all people through the gifts, talents, and provisions He has given us. Transformed giving is when we look beyond our finances and realize that we are to be living sacrificially. Our hearts, our prayers, and our time go along with each dollar we give. That is the only way to be the cheerful giver God has called us to be. And His Spirit will help us to become that person.

In the book of Romans, Paul wrote about the believers in Jerusalem who were suffering. Motivated by love, he took up an "offering" from the Christians in Macedonia and Achaia (Romans 15:26). The word Paul used for offering is the same Greek word for communion or fellowship. The Lord used Paul's heart and the people's gifts to bless those in need and to bless the givers. Giving is yet another aspect of living the contented life.

A SHARING LIFE

After Jesus died on the cross, He was buried in the tomb and rose again three days later. The book of Acts tells us He continued appearing to the apostles for a period of forty days, proving to them He was alive and talking to them about the kingdom of God (Acts 1:3). Since these were Jesus' last days on earth with His followers, they were most likely hanging on every word He said. At the end of the forty days, Jesus met with His disciples one last time in person. His final words were recorded in Matthew 28.

> Jesus came and told his disciples, "I have been given all authority in heaven and on earth. Therefore, go

and make disciples of all the nations, baptizing them in the name of the Father and the Son and the Holy Spirit. Teach these new disciples to obey all the commands I have given you. And be sure of this: I am with you always, even to the end of the age."

Matthew 28:18–20

God's heart for His creation is communion and restoration. He created us in His image and likeness. Accepting this as our reality results in realizing our purpose to fulfill Jesus' final words, referred to as the Great Commission. Speaking of God's heart for redemption, reconciliation, and communion, John the Beloved penned this famous passage:

For this is how God loved the world: He gave his one and only Son, so that everyone who believes in him will not perish but have eternal life.

John 3:16

God the Father wants us to return to Him, to be restored to what He originally intended. He wants this for each and every person on the entire earth. God's plan for redemption began all the way back in the garden of Eden immediately following the fall. The first gospel message, the Good News, is recorded in Genesis 3:

Then the LORD God said to the serpent, because you have done this, you are cursed more than all animals, domestic and wild. You will crawl on your belly, groveling in the dust as long as you live. And I will cause hostility between you and the woman, and between your offspring and her offspring. He will strike your head, and you will strike his heel.

Genesis 3:14–15

Picture Adam and Eve living within God's perfect creation. One day as Eve is taking a stroll, Satan, disguised as a serpent, approaches her and questions the intent of her Creator God. *Did God really say that?* Satan placed the doubt and deception in Eve's mind, causing her to wonder, *Is God withholding something from me? Does God really know what's best for my life?* So she ate the fruit and offered it to her husband, Adam, who did the same.

Every time Satan is mentioned in the Bible, he is either disguising himself, questioning God's character, or trying to separate mankind from communion with God. In this Genesis passage, we see him doing all three. After Adam and Eve ate the fruit, Satan thought he had won. He thought he had damaged man's relationship with God beyond repair. Thankfully, he was wrong, for these verses reveal both the problem of sin and God's redemptive plan.

Genesis 3:14–15 states there will be an ongoing hostility between Satan and God's creation. We see this hostility continuing today. Satan does not want you or your family to discover God's true purpose or experience the fullness God wants for your life. Satan will do everything in his power to prevent you from fulfilling God's will.

This is sin and the problem of sin. It will keep you at enmity with God, which is exactly what Satan wants.

In verse 15 of Genesis 3, God's redemption plan—the Good News—is vividly portrayed with these words:

> He will strike your head, and you will strike his heel.

Referring to the offspring of the woman, God says "He" will strike the serpent's head. The woman's offspring is Jesus, the "promised seed" (Galatians 4:4). Jesus will be victorious because He will strike the serpent's head. But Satan, the serpent, will only strike Jesus' heel. Satan was not successful in his attempt to defeat God because Jesus rose from the dead. What Satan intended as his final victory in his battle with God—Jesus' crucifixion—God proved victorious in Satan's defeat. Speaking of Jesus and His victory on the cross, Paul wrote this:

> He canceled the record of the charges against us and took it away by nailing it to the cross. In this way, he disarmed the spiritual rulers and authorities. He shamed them publicly by his victory over them on the cross.
>
> *Colossians 2:14–15*

God's promise of redemption, restoration, victory, and a coming Savior began in Genesis and continues today for all who believe. The entire Old Testament looked forward with prophecies and promises of the coming King, and the entire New Testament looks back at His life, death, and resurrection with continued promises of new life for all who believe.

After man sinned, God did not leave Adam and Eve, His precious creation, wondering if they would be left to their fallen state and fate of curses. He met them there in their brokenness and shame and promised redemption instead. How overwhelming, humbling, and joyous this moment must have been. They had disobeyed God and eaten of the fruit, falling into the trap of Satan himself. Yet God, in His mercy, met them there and promised He would restore them back to His original glorious plan of peace.

What would it have been like for Adam and Eve had they not had this assurance of future good? What would their lives have been like without this promise to cling to? Hopeless.

That desperate feeling of hopelessness is what people around us are experiencing each and every day. They are lost. Without God's promises, there is nothing but despair.

The book of Job tells the story of a righteous man who lost everything—his home, his children, his wealth, and his livelihood. Listen to what he said about hopelessness:

> For what is the hope of the godless when he is cut off, when God requires his life?
>
> *Job 27:8*

There is no hope apart from Christ. This is the truth of the gospel. This is the reality of our world.

All believers have been commissioned to share the gospel to the ends of the earth. But the fact is, few do. There are many excuses, and many find their root in fear. People fear rejection, losing friends, income sources, or jobs. But the only proper fear is the fear of the Lord.

The psalmist said:

> How joyful are those who fear the LORD—all who follow his ways! You will enjoy the fruit of your labor. How joyful and prosperous you will be!
>
> *Psalm 128:1–2*

Shortly after Jesus' ascension into heaven, while the believers were gathered in one place, the promised Holy Spirit came to the disciples. This is called the Day of Pentecost, and it is outlined in Acts 2:1–31. The disciples were suddenly filled with the Holy Spirit and began glorifying God in languages not their own. Devout Jews from many different regions were in Jerusalem for Pentecost at this time, and all were amazed to hear these men speaking in his own native tongue. The crowd increased, and Peter, filled with the Holy Spirit, began to preach. The book of Acts tells us that three thousand people were saved and added to the church that day.

God's will and purpose for your life is that you too would be a part of the glorious plan of sharing the Good News of Jesus with the world around you. That doesn't mean you have to preach to a crowd of three thousand, like Peter did. That doesn't even mean you have to become a pastor and teach a congregation every Sunday, like I do.

Instead, allow God's love to pour into your life and out of your life, affecting those in it. The fragrance of Christ flowing through your life will give others hope, a glimpse that perhaps there is something more. Maybe the refreshingly honest way you conduct business will draw others to want to work with you and learn from you. Maybe the loving relationship you have with your spouse or your children will draw people to you to learn to have the same. Maybe the way you joyfully give your time and your finances, however God leads, will bless and inspire people to serve God and others. The nature of God's love is to be shared.

Whatever your unique gifts and talents may be, it is God's desire for you to use them for His glory. God will open doors for you to share His love and hope with those around you.

THE
CONDUCT OF
THE CONTENTED LIFE

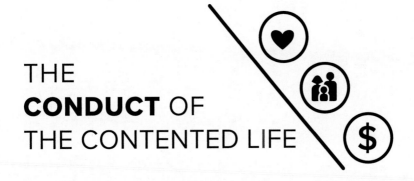

"THE CHRISTIAN IDEAL HAS NOT BEEN TRIED
AND FOUND WANTING. IT HAS BEEN FOUND
DIFFICULT; AND LEFT UNTRIED."[20]

G. K. CHESTERTON

Following my lunch with Pastor Carl back in 1992, I felt a strong urge to attend the School of Ministry at Calvary Chapel Costa Mesa. This school is typically attended by those who would like to become pastors. I, on the other hand, was a young believer with a thriving business who had no intention of changing occupations. My company provided a good source of income for my family, and I was enjoying the newfound freedom of doing business according to God's principles.

Attending the School of Ministry was clearly God's plan for me. My faith grew exponentially during those two years. After graduating, the Lord brought me a business partner who helped free up my time to do ministry. God opened many doors for me and my wife to serve at our church. We worked in the high school ministry, and I became the surf coach and began teaching Bible studies at some of the local high schools in Orange County. Owning my business enabled me to give generously to the church, and I thoroughly enjoyed participating as a chaperone on mission trips for the younger generation.

We were truly experiencing the contented life that is only found in Christ.

In the midst of this blessed season, my wife was diagnosed with breast cancer. Our world was turned upside down. Looking back, I can see the hand of God guiding our family through every year, from when I was hungover in Mexico to when I joined the School of Ministry. It was a miracle God had held my family, my marriage, and even my business together through the tumult of my own stupidity. We were stronger for it and learning a new kind of grace from God to get us through tough times as believers.

The Bible has much to say about suffering. Contrary to what some teach from the pulpit, we are not handed a get-out-of-jail-free card when we become Christians. In fact, we are promised afflictions and sufferings. The psalmist said this:

> Many are the afflictions of the righteous, but the LORD delivers him out of them all.
>
> *Psalm 34:19 NKJV*

Writing to the church in Corinth, Paul said:

> I want to know Christ and experience the mighty power that raised him from the dead. I want to suffer with him, sharing in his death, so that one way or another I will experience the resurrection from the dead!
>
> *Philippians 3:10–11*

Are you experiencing a season of hardship in your life? Is your family falling apart due to your own poor choices or the choices of others? Is your marriage on rocky ground? Are you working through turmoil in your workplace?

Every person will go through affliction at some point in their lives. We are promised suffering, but that's not all we are promised. In the midst of trials, God is with us. The Lord takes on our pain, as He did on the cross, so that we are able to experience His joy in every circumstance. We learn more about who He is, and He helps us become who we were always meant to be. We grow closer to Jesus, who suffered more than any man, because He is the only one who can provide everything we need to survive. We partake in His death on the cross when we walk through experiences of death in our own lives: the death of a loved one, a terminal diagnosis, a failed relationship, the loss of a home or job. We don't have to go through these dark times alone. Christians have the promise of *Jehovah Shammah*, "the Lord is there." Walking through these pains of death enables us to die to ourselves as Christ did. Furthermore, it enables us to experience the power of the resurrection whereby Christ Himself was raised from the dead.

Wouldn't you love to have that same power alive and well within your relationships today? The promise for every believer is this—you will.

During my wife's battle with cancer, our family received an outpouring of blessings from our church. This love, comfort, and support came in the form of help, prayer, and understanding. Unfortunately, this is not the experience for every believer. Many have entered into relationships with the church, a Christian business partner, a spouse who claimed to love God, or Jesus followers who promised friendship, only to be let down over and over again. If you have not experienced this situation in the church yourself, it is likely only a matter of time until you will.

There are all kinds of people within churches today. Imagine a place filled with the most anointed of teachers, then imagine a place filled with the worst of sinners. Think about the outcasts and the darlings of society, those with a history of integrity and those with a history of deceit. You will find them all in the church.

This is perhaps the greatest Christian paradox: we are all perfected, justified, forgiven, and set free to be the person God has called us to be,

But we are also still sinners.

"Christ died for the ungodly …" (Romans 5:6) "… of whom I am chief" (1 Timothy 1:15). These are direct quotes from the apostle Paul, but they are statements every one of us could claim.

The church is the place where we all come together to be set free from our past, set apart for good works, and sent out for God's purpose.

God wants to restore His image and likeness to the church and believers all over the world, including you and me. In order to do this, God has asked us to partner with Him as we participate, encourage, exhort, teach, correct, and live side by side with fellow believers and non-believers alike. When I talk about the church, I'm not talking about a building full of people. I'm talking about all those who have been saved by God's grace through the death and resurrection of His Son Jesus. These are the called and the chosen whom God wants to use—flaws and all—as His witnesses all over the world. This group and body of believers regularly comes together to worship God, pray for one another, encourage one another, and learn from one another before going back out into the world to share the hope of God that is within them.

It is beautiful, incredible, and *messy.*

During the past fifteen years of being a pastor, I have learned a secret. This thing called church only works when we have an attitude of humility and submission. And this applies as well to our families, our workplaces, and our homes. We must be Christlike in word and deed. The key to the contented life is communion with Christ. On this principle hangs everything else, including our relationships with others. This verse sums up why very well:

And further, submit to one another out of reverence
for Christ.

Ephesians 5:21

This simple sentence helps us to understand how God
wants us to relate to others. This verse acts as a hinge to show
us how to view and conduct ourselves in our relationships.
When we are motivated by deep admiration for Christ, we
can sacrifice selfishness and submit to others. This can only
be accomplished when we allow the Holy Spirit to be present
and at work in us, for the Holy Spirit is the hinge that opens
the door for a Third Person to enter into our relationship. That
Third Person is Christ Himself.

The apostle John wrote:

My little children, I am writing these things to you so
that you may not sin. But if anyone does sin, we have
an *advocate* with the Father, Jesus Christ the righteous.

1 John 2:1, emphasis mine

The word *advocate* in Greek is *parakletos*, which means,
"called to one's aid" or "one who advocates for another … the
word denotes one who acts on an another's behalf as a medi-
ator, an intercessor, or an encourager. In 1 John 2:1, Christ is
called the *paraclete* because He represents people to God."[21]

Jesus used the word parakletos this way:

If you love me, you will keep my commandments.
And I will ask the Father, and he will give you another
Helper (Parakletos), to be with you forever, even
the Spirit of truth, whom the world cannot receive,
because it neither sees him nor knows him. You know
him, for he dwells with you and will be in you.

John 14:15–17

Reading these two verses really brings clarity to what Solomon wrote:

> A person standing alone can be attacked and defeated, but two can stand back-to-back and conquer. Three are even better, for a triple-braided cord is not easily broken.
>
> *Ecclesiastes 4:12*

The cure for conflict with one another is to know that Jesus is present as the Third *Person* in every relationship. It is not merely an issue of "what I want" versus "what you want." The primary concern becomes "what does Christ want?" Before we do anything, we must ask if it is what Jesus would have us to do.

If we do not recognize Jesus as the Third Person in our relationships, then we naturally only see two people involved. Our pride overpowers us, and we refuse to submit to one another. We claim, "I am right, and they are wrong," and we wait for the other to give in first. We begin to rationalize things in our minds, driven by self-justification, and the conflict rages on.

But when we recognize we are not alone, we no longer worry about who is right or wrong. When we recognize the involvement of the Third Person in our lives, we fix our concerns on what He wants for us. When we come to this place in our relationships with one another, the Holy Spirit empowers us to follow His example.

> For God called you to do good, even if it means suffering, just as Christ suffered for you. He is your example, and you must follow in his steps.
>
> *1 Peter 2:21*

Forgiveness

Because we have received forgiveness *from* Christ for our sins, we are then able to enter into this beautiful place of communion *with* Christ. But we must pass through this doorway of forgiveness before we can truly experience this kind of intimacy. The writer of Hebrews said this:

> And so, dear brothers and sisters, we can boldly enter heaven's Most Holy Place because of the blood of Jesus.
>
> *Hebrews 10:19*

The apostle Paul, writing to the Ephesians, said this:

> But now you have been united with Christ Jesus. Once you were far away from God, but now you have been brought near to him through the blood of Christ. For Christ himself has brought peace to us.
>
> *Ephesians 2:13–14a*

We only can look forward to heaven because of the blood of Jesus. Yes, we exercise faith, or belief, unto salvation, but Paul tells us that even faith is a gift from God.

> But God is so rich in mercy, and he loved us so much, that even though we were dead because of our sins, he gave us life when he raised Christ from the dead. (It is only by God's grace that you have been saved!)
>
> *Ephesians 2:4–5*

> God saved you by his grace when you believed. And you can't take credit for this; it is a gift from God. Salvation is not a reward for the good things we have done, so none of us can boast about it.
>
> *Ephesians 2:8–9*

God's original intent was for forgiveness to be received by the whole world. This mission and ministry of Jesus while here on earth was to give His life as a ransom for many (Mark 10:45), to call sinners to repentance (Luke 5:31–32), and to give eternal life (John 3:16). John 3:16 says, "God so loved the world." It does not say God loved the good people in the world, God loved the least sinful people in the world, or God loved the hard workers in the world. No, God loved the whole world. Jesus died for the whole world. His forgiveness, His love, and His sacrifice are available to all who believe in Jesus.

This is important for us to remember as we move into experiencing communion with Christ in our relationships. Jesus not only forgave you for your sinful behavior, He forgave your spouse too. God's desire is for you to take the forgiveness He has freely given to you—the forgiveness that has opened the door for you to have communion with Christ—and extend that same forgiveness to others. Just as God is working in and through you, changing you from the inside out, He is changing those around you who love Him as well.

> *So we have stopped evaluating others from a human point of view.* At one time we thought of Christ merely from a human point of view. How differently we know him now! This means that anyone who belongs to Christ has become a new person. The old life is gone; a new life has begun! And all of this is a gift from God, who brought us back to himself through Christ.
>
> *And God has given us this task of reconciling people to him. For God was in Christ, reconciling the world to himself, no longer counting people's sins against them. And he gave us this wonderful message of reconciliation. So we are Christ's ambassadors; God is making his appeal through us.*

We speak for Christ when we plead, "Come back to God!" For God made Christ, who never sinned, to be the offering for our sin, so that we could be made right with God through Christ.

2 Corinthians 5:16–21, emphasis mine

Jesus Himself also gave His followers a warning regarding forgiveness:

If you forgive those who sin against you, your heavenly Father will forgive you. But if you refuse to forgive others, your Father will not forgive your sins.

Matthew 6:14–15

In order to really understand the strong stance Jesus takes on the importance of forgiveness, let's look at a parable on forgiveness that He shared with His disciples:

Therefore, the Kingdom of Heaven can be compared to a king who decided to bring his accounts up to date with servants who had borrowed money from him. In the process, one of his debtors was brought in who owed him millions of dollars. He couldn't pay, so his master ordered that he be sold—along with his wife, his children, and everything he owned—to pay the debt.

But the man fell down before his master and begged him, "Please, be patient with me, and I will pay it all." Then his master was filled with pity for him, and he released him and forgave his debt.

But when the man left the king, he went to a fellow servant who owed him a few thousand dollars. He grabbed him by the throat and demanded instant payment.

His fellow servant fell down before him and begged for a little more time. "Be patient with me, and I will pay it," he pleaded. But his creditor wouldn't wait. He had the man arrested and put in prison until the debt could be paid in full.

When some of the other servants saw this, they were very upset. They went to the king and told him everything that had happened. Then the king called in the man he had forgiven and said, "You evil servant! I forgave you that tremendous debt because you pleaded with me. Shouldn't you have mercy on your fellow servant, just as I had mercy on you?" Then the angry king sent the man to prison to be tortured until he had paid his entire debt.

That's what my heavenly Father will do to you if you refuse to forgive your brothers and sisters from your heart.

Matthew 18:23–35

As forgiveness has been freely given to us, we must freely forgive others. Paul wrote:

Get rid of all bitterness, rage, anger, harsh words, and slander, as well as all types of evil behavior. Instead, be kind to each other, tenderhearted, *forgiving one another, just as God through Christ has forgiven you.*

Ephesians 4:31–32, emphasis mine

We forgive because God, through Christ, has forgiven us.

We forgive in the same way that God, through Christ, has forgiven us.

So often we use forgiveness as a means of controlling reconciliation. We say things like, "I will talk to him again when he apologizes or asks for forgiveness. I will forgive her when she starts acting differently or when I can tell she has really changed."

While we have been given Christ's ministry of reconciliation (2 Corinthians 5:16–21), we are not required to reconcile all relationships. Reconciliation should always be our aim; however, it is not always possible and is most often a process. Forgiveness can be given with or without reconciliation. Let's look at how and when Christ forgave us:

> But God showed his great love for us by sending Christ to die for us *while we were still sinners.*
>
> *Romans 5:8, emphasis mine*

God made forgiveness available to us while we were still sinners, indicating we did not deserve it or earn it. This also makes it clear that God forgave us before we knew we needed His forgiveness or had even asked for it. This is how we are to forgive others.

Peter asked the question many of us wonder:

> "Lord, how often should I forgive someone who sins against me? Seven times?"
>
> "No, not seven times," Jesus replied, "but seventy times seven!"
>
> *Matthew 18:21–22*

I'm sure Peter was as shocked as we are at that response. Who could possibly keep count of that many offenses? No one! This was exactly the point Jesus was making—we should not keep count of how many times we have to forgive others because Jesus does not keep count of how many times He has forgiven us. How grateful we are for that!

We will never overcome the hurts and pains we have experienced at the hands of others until we are able to show God's forgiveness. We will never be able to forgive as Christ has forgiven us until we are motivated by the love of God.

> Either way, Christ's love controls us. Since we believe that Christ died for all, we also believe that we have all died to our old life.
>
> *2 Corinthians 5:14*

> Love is patient and kind. Love is not jealous or boastful or proud or rude. It does not demand its own way. It is not irritable, and it keeps no record of being wronged. It does not rejoice about injustice but rejoices whenever the truth wins out. Love never gives up, never loses faith, is always hopeful, and endures through every circumstance.
>
> *1 Corinthians 13:4–7*

> Most important of all, continue to show deep love for each other, for love covers a multitude of sins.
>
> *1 Peter 4:8*

Only when we are controlled by the love of Christ can we forgive as He forgives and love as He loves. Only when we allow the Holy Spirit to fill us can we show deep love for one another and allow this love to cover sins.

God wants to give you hope in the midst of your current relationships with your spouse, your children, your colleagues, even with other believers—challenges and all. But it will not be easy. You will need to continue to press into those foundations of the faith as we journey onward. God is more than able to bring healing, wholeness, and joy to the most broken relationships. And He is able to use you, an unworthy servant, to bring Him glory and to work in spite of your shortcomings.

In this next section, I will be sharing encouraging stories and narratives which testify to God's ability to create beauty from broken situations and relationships. I have purposely included testimonies that fit into the boxes we'd like them to, as well as some that don't follow the storyline we would have expected or hoped for. In all of them, God is good. In all of them, people have learned what I hope you too will discover: The key to the contented life is communion with Christ.

IN OUR MARRIAGES

> According to the Bible, the marriage act is more than a physical act. It is an act of sharing. It is an act of communion. It is an act of total self-giving wherein the husband gives himself completely to the wife, and the wife gives herself to the husband in such a way that the two actually become one flesh.[22]
>
> *Wayne Mack*

On September 30, 2018, my wife and I celebrated forty years of marriage. After four decades of experience and more than twenty years of counseling others, I can say without a doubt that the marriage union produces the greatest delights and the deepest sorrows. It is the place wherein many single people believe they will find the most satisfaction and the place many married people find the most distress.

So it doesn't surprise me when I read the statistics on divorce in the United States—forty to fifty percent—and in the wealthier communities, that percentage increases to seventy. Marriage is hard work. But why is it so difficult?

We find the answer to that question in creation. Every time I read the Genesis 1 account, my eyes always gravitate to this repeated phrase: "And God saw that it was good." After every day of creation, we read that phrase, but when we get to the sixth day, it changes. After God created Adam, we read, "Then God looked over all he had made, and he saw that it was *very good!*" (Genesis 1:30, emphasis mine).

God placed Adam in the garden of Eden where he worked and lived in harmony with the Lord. Eden was to be the happiest place on the planet. The garden provided all he needed in terms of food and shelter, but it appears that Adam wasn't happy.

> Then the LORD God said, "It is not good for the man to be alone, I will make a helper who is just right for him."
>
> *Genesis 2:18*

> So the LORD God caused the man to fall into a deep sleep. While the man slept, the LORD God took out one of the man's ribs and closed up the opening. Then the LORD God made a woman from the rib, and he brought her to the man. "At last!" the man exclaimed. "This one is bone from my bone, and flesh from my flesh! She will be called 'woman,' because she was taken from 'man.'" This explains why a man leaves his father and mother and is joined to his wife, and the two are united into one.
>
> *Genesis 2:21–24*

It appears that Adam wasn't satisfied being single, so God provided someone, "just right for him." How do you know when someone is just right for you? You will know when God brings them to you.

I was eighteen years old when I met Teresa. I vividly remember the first time I saw her. We were both working in a mall—she at a hot dog stand, me at a men's clothing store. One hot summer day, I was walking down the mall when I saw this tall, beautiful blonde with piercing blue eyes standing behind the counter. My heart melted. I couldn't take my eyes off of her. It took me a week or two to get enough courage to ask her out. When I finally mustered up enough nerve, she said "NO!" I was crushed. Thankfully, God had a different plan. We went out on our first date on September 30, 1977, and were married a year later.

We exchanged vows in a quaint little Lutheran Church in Chico, California. At that time, I was not a Christian, but Teresa was … kind of. The ceremony was beautiful, but the most beautiful part was when Teresa's cousin Rick sang this amazing song. It didn't mean anything to me then, but it means everything to me today. Here are the words.

> He is now to be among you, at the calling of your heart. Rest assured this troubadour is acting on His part. The union of your spirits here has caused Him to remain. For whenever two or more of you are gathered in His name, there is love, there is love. Well, a man shall leave his mother and a woman leave her home. They shall travel on to where the two shall be as one. As it was in the beginning is now until the end. A woman draws her life from man and gives it back again, and there is love, there is love. Well then, what's to be the reason for becoming man and wife? Is it love that brings you here or love that gives you life? For if loving is the answer then who's the giving for? Do you believe in something that you've never seen before? Oh, there's love, oh, there's love. Oh,

the marriage of your spirits here has caused Him to remain. For whenever two or more of you are gathered in His name, there is love, oh, there's love.[23]

As I think back on that day and remember these lyrics, I am so blessed to know, without a doubt, that God brought Teresa to me. Admittedly, our marriage has not always been a picture of marital bliss. We experienced good times, yes, but those first twelve years of marriage as non-believers were more like a marital mess.

What made our marriage a mess? Why didn't we experience martial bliss? One word: SIN!

Recall our discussion in the first section regarding the first sin of Adam and Eve. They were living in a perfect world, with a perfect job, a perfect home, and a perfect family. Yet they were still deceived, and they sinned.

Even within our marriages—unions most of us chose voluntarily and vowed to stick to, until death do us part—sin manages to creep in, much like the serpent did. It deceives us into believing that God is withholding something from us or that we know better than God what is good and right for our lives.

This wrong way of thinking is the root cause of discontentment in marriages.

I have had the privilege of officiating many marriage ceremonies. As I prepare for the wedding, I always want to go back to the beginning. I can almost see Adam and Eve standing before God, facing one another hand in hand, in the midst of the garden of Eden. I can almost hear the distant sound of the rushing waters from the rivers through the garden and a host of heavenly angels singing, "He is now to be among you, at the calling of your hearts," as God was there officiating the very first wedding.

This first ceremony was not only special to Adam and Eve, it was very special to God. This would be the first divine institution God made for mankind, which I believe was on the mind of the apostle Paul when he wrote these words to the church in Ephesus.

> Therefore a man shall leave his father and mother and hold fast to his wife, and the two shall become one flesh. This mystery is profound, and I am saying that it refers to Christ and the church.
>
> *Ephesians 5:31–32 ESV*

The word *mystery* in the Bible is defined as "something that once was hidden but now has been unveiled in Scripture."

God created marriage to be the first biblical institution for specific reasons. It shows its priority above every other relationship, and it is a picture and foreshadowing of the relationship between believers (the church) and the church's groom (Christ). In the marriage relationship, the Third Person is needed. As I said earlier, the hinge that opens the door is the Holy Spirit, and the Door, or the Third Person, is Christ.

> I am the door. If anyone enters by Me, he will be saved and will go in and out and find pasture.
>
> *John 10:9 NKJV*

Jesus said this regarding the Holy Spirit:

> I am telling you these things now while I am still with you. But when the Father sends the Advocate as my representative—that is, the Holy Spirit—he will teach you everything and will remind you of everything I have told you. I am leaving you with a gift—peace of mind and heart. And the peace I give is a gift the world cannot give. So don't be troubled or afraid.
>
> *John 14:25–27*

Paul uses the passage in Genesis that speaks of the marriage relationship and applies it to an entirely different relationship, that of Christ and His church. This is why Satan is so merciless in attacking marriages; he is always at work to destroy this beautiful picture. The Bible says this of God's enemy:

> Stay alert! Watch out for your great enemy, the devil. He prowls around like a roaring lion, looking for someone to devour.
>
> *1 Peter 5:8*

Peter compares the devil to a roaring lion. That is an interesting metaphor especially in light of an article I read titled, "When Mountain Lions Hunt, They Prey on the Weak." The article states, "Predators do not always play fair. Sometimes they choose their victims based on physical condition, preferring young, old, sick or injured prey. That is the idea, although surprisingly it has not been tested much. But now researchers have found that one predator does, in fact, show a preference for less-than-fully-capable victims. The findings may have implication for the spread of chronic wasting disease among deer populations."[24]

The devil doesn't play fair. He chooses victims based on their spiritual condition, preferring young, old, or injured prey, preferring those couples who are less-than-fully-capable to attack. And like the deer populations, divorce has spread through the human population at an alarming rate.

If you are married, consider how this looks in relation to your marriage. Are their areas where you and your spouse are spiritually weak? Areas where you feel less-than-fully-capable? Stay alert and watch out! Sin creeps into these vulnerable areas where the enemy will readily attack.

This vulnerability applies to the church as well. Satan loves to attack His Bride and create division. But the church should be the place where we come together with other believers in fellowship or communion. This can be challenging because people are sinners. But as a people who are saved, sanctified, and redeemed by God, we must work together as He would have us to do. There will be tensions in these relationships as we learn how to walk alongside one another. But through all of this, we are becoming living examples of God's mercy, grace, and long-suffering as forgiveness and reconciliation take place.

Marriage between a husband and wife is much like the relationship described above. In addition to the *agapē* (unconditional) love and *phileo* (friendship) love, in marriage we add *eros* (sexual) love. The intimacy within marriage brings the relationship to an entirely different level than that which we experience with our fellow believers. This intimate relationship between a husband and wife is where the oneness comes in. The two are joined together in body, soul (mind), and spirit. This is how the church is to be joined together with Christ:

In our bodies:

> And so, dear brothers and sisters, I plead with you to give your bodies to God because of all that he has done for you. Let them be a living and holy sacrifice—the kind he will find acceptable. This is truly the way to worship him.
>
> *Romans 12:1*

In our souls (minds):

> Let this mind be in you which was also in Christ Jesus, who, being in the form of God, did not consider it robbery to be equal with God, but made Himself

of no reputation, taking the form of a bondservant, and coming in the likeness of men. And being found in appearance as a man, He humbled Himself and became obedient to the point of death, even the death of the cross.

Philippians 2:5–8 NKJV

In our spirits:

Don't you realize that your bodies are actually parts of Christ? Should a man take his body, which is part of Christ, and join it to a prostitute? Never! And don't you realize that if a man joins himself to a prostitute, he becomes one body with her? For the Scriptures say, "The two are united into one." But the person who is joined to the Lord is one spirit with him.

1 Corinthians 6:15–17

This type of relationship, where the two are so entwined that there is no dividing them, was God's design for marriage when He first created it. It's a relationship so pure that the arms of the other bring comfort in pain and encouragement in hard times, so safe that each can thrive in their unique talents and differences while supporting and cheering the other on, and so loving that they each feel the freedom to become the person God has called them to be as individuals and as one.

Too many couples are not experiencing this in their marriages. I believe this is largely due to the mindset of our western culture. We value self and the individual above others or the family. Marriage is not considered a holy institution formed by God that no man should tear apart. It's a tax write-off for some and a temporary next step in the relationship for others. This is no doubt the result of sin in our fallen world.

Consider the mystery of marriage from the Creator's perspective.

> It is interesting to compare the church to the first bride in the Bible, Eve. She was taken from Adam's side, and Christ's side was pierced for us on the cross. She was formed when Adam was asleep, and Christ experienced the sleep of death to create the church. Eve shared Adam's nature, and the church partakes of Christ's nature. Eve was the object of her mate's love and care, and Christ loves the church and cares for it. Adam was willing to become a sinner because of his love for his wife, and Christ willingly was made sin because of His love for the church. Eve was formed and brought to Adam before sin entered the human family; the church was in the mind and heart of God before the foundation of the world.[25]

Marriage is a mystery indeed.

So, how do we enter into this sacred place of communion in our relationships with our spouses? How do we invite the Third Person, Jesus, into our marriages? How do we begin the process of allowing God to change our relationships and our habits for His glory and for our good?

The book of Ephesians gives us some practical advice on how husbands should treat wives and how wives should treat husbands. Through my years of marital counseling, however, I have found many hurt spouses often use these verses to point fingers at how the other should be acting. I do not believe Paul or the Holy Spirit intended these Scriptures to be used as a rating tool for your spouse. Paul, speaking under the authority of the Holy Spirit, was addressing the individual. Husbands, if you are a husband, this section is for you to read. Wives, if you are a wife, this section is for you to read. Allow God's Word to speak to you by being humble and willing to hear it. Examine yourself by God's Word and ask yourself, "Am I doing these things?" Invite the Holy Spirit into this discussion. "God, are there areas where I am not _____ my wife/husband?"

> And further, submit to one another out of reverence for Christ. For wives, this means you are to submit to your husbands as to the Lord. For the husband is the head of his wife as Christ is the head of the church. He is the Savior of His body, the church. As the church submits to Christ, so you wives should submit to your husbands in everything.
>
> For husbands, this means you are to love your wives just as Christ loved the church. He gave up His life for her to make her holy and clean, washed by the cleansing of God's Word. He did this to present her to Himself as a glorious church, without a spot or wrinkle or any other blemish. Instead, she will be holy and without fault. In the same way, husbands ought to love their wives as they love their own bodies. For a man who loves his wife actually shows love for himself. No one hates his own body but feeds and cares for it, just as Christ cares for the church. And we are members of his body.
>
> As the Scriptures say, "A man leaves his father and mother and is joined to his wife, and the two are united into one." This is a great mystery, but it is an illustration of the way Christ and the church are one. So again I say, each man must love his wife as he loves himself, and the wife must respect her husband.
>
> *Ephesians 5:21–33*

These Scriptures are not suggestions on how to treat your spouse, they are actually *commands*. Our marriages are meant to be a picture of God's love for us—a representation of Christ's love for the church. When we look at these Scriptures with that understanding, we see that collectively the bride of Christ should submit to Christ. We do this willingly and lovingly because of the authority God has given the Son (Philippians 2:9–11) and because of all He has done for us.

Likewise, Christ loves us and has loved us by washing us clean through His Word and through the giving up of His life for us on the cross. What an incredible gift.

When we allow Christ to be at the center of our marriages, we experience the joy and freedom that comes from following our God-given callings within them. It is the giving and receiving of God's love within marriages that keeps them strong and healthy. It is this kind of love the world cannot tear apart, a love orchestrated by Christ Himself.

In order to experience communion with our spouses, we must first experience communion with Christ. This is where it all begins. Communion with Christ doesn't mean a rosy path of marital bliss that removes discontentment from your marriage. Perfection isn't promised, but completeness is. The safest place you can be on this planet and in your marriage is when you are both experiencing daily communion with Christ. It is within this relationship you will find everything you are searching for.

Love Lost and Found Again

A dear friend of mine was married for nearly thirty years. She and her husband professed to be Christians. While her husband knew the Scriptures, his heart was not motivated by love. He was legalistic, which only produced hypocrisy. She endured much suffering over the years but chose to stay and submit to him because she believed this was what God's Word instructed her to do. One day, she discovered her husband was having multiple affairs. Hurt and confused, she left her house and ran away. Instead of running away from God, she drew closer to Him, throwing herself completely upon His mercies. During one of her quiet times in communion with Christ, she felt the urging of the Holy Spirit to return to her husband in spite of the betrayal and circumstances. So she did.

Over the course of time, more issues in the marriage were revealed. As more hurts and more betrayals were uncovered, she would leave her house and run away, each time running closer to God. Time and time again, she felt the Lord urging her to return to her husband.

As she later described these experiences to me, it was clear her decisions to run away and return were more than instant reactions to being hurt. She didn't run away, feel guilty, then go back. She wrestled through these decisions with much agony and tears. The guilt and shame she felt over her situation was palpable. She believed God hated divorce and did not want to tear apart what God had joined together (Matthew 19:5). She hoped God would bring the necessary healing for the relationship to mend and move forward.

Sadly, her husband continued to harden his heart, and their marriage ultimately ended in divorce.

Around this time, there was a man in our church fellowship in the midst of a similar situation. He and his wife had been married for over two decades. They had been attending church together for years, but their marriage was miserable. His wife was unwilling to submit to him and had never made it easy for him to be the man God had called him to be. Sadly, their marriage also ended in divorce.

The woman in the first story and the man in the second story began a friendship, which blossomed into romance over time. They came to me for counseling regarding their new-found relationship. I had known them both personally for a long time but was surprised at this news. I was concerned they were attracted to their shared experiences more than to each other, a red flag in any relationship. Rather than dismiss it, we decided to pray. Could God be drawing these two people together? Would God choose to bring them together in this way at this time? I wasn't sure.

Shortly after that prayer, these words from the prophet Isaiah came to mind:

> "My thoughts are nothing like your thoughts," says the LORD. "And my ways are far beyond anything you could imagine. For just as the heavens are higher than the earth, so my ways are higher than your ways and my thoughts higher than your thoughts."
>
> *Isaiah 55:8–9*

I am amazed at how the Lord brought this couple together and carried them through some of their darkest days to find God and each other on the other side. They have been married for a few years now, constantly serving one another, submitting to one another, loving one another, and inviting the Third Person into each and every part of their relationship. In spite of their past hardships, they are experiencing communion with Christ and with one another in their marriage.

Divorce

Divorce is a sword that doesn't cut swiftly or precisely between the husband and wife. Two lives had become one, and the separation line cannot be clean. Divorce hurts anyone and everyone in its way. Don't think for a second that divorce is the easiest option for your situation. It is a wrecking ball ready to damage and destroy.

I think too many people use the statement "God hates divorce" (Malachi 2:16) with ill intent. Using it as a reason to stay married is respectable, but using it to shame or penalize those in difficult marriages or divorced never is. God hates divorce, but He also hates hard hearts (Matthew 19:8). I am in no way condoning divorce. I have seen many friends go through this horrendous time of tearing apart and understand why God hates it. Those who have been in situations where they felt like divorce was their only choice need prayers and sympathy, not judgment.

We live in a fallen world. We see the effects of sin around us every day in our relationships. No matter what your circumstances are, whether you've experienced divorce or are in the midst of one, God has a plan for you still.

Love Unveiled

On our trip to Israel in 1992, we met a couple that was not happily married. The woman was a born again believer who loved the Lord. The man was not a believer but loved his wife. There was great tension between them at times. He had no interest in spiritual things or in being around other believers. While he seemed unhappy and even sad, she seemed happy. Despite their obvious differences and tension in the relationship, I never heard her nag or provoke him toward spiritual things. She appeared to be loving and respectful to her husband constantly.

Many years later, I was walking through the courtyard of a local church when a man approached me. "Jeff, how are you?" he asked. I didn't recognize him at first. He looked familiar, but I couldn't place him until he said, "I've been born again!" I recognized him then as the unhappy man from Israel. I asked him what happened to cause this change in him. He replied, "My wife won me over by her love for Christ." My heart was truly filled with joy.

Whenever I think about this couple, I am reminded of the following Scriptures from 1 Peter:

> For God called you to do good, even if it means suffering, just as Christ suffered for you. He is your example, and you must follow in his steps.
>
> *1 Peter 2:21*

> In the same way, you wives must accept the authority of your husbands. Then, even if some refuse to obey the Good News, your godly lives will speak to them without any words. They will be won over by observing your pure and reverent lives.
>
> *1 Peter 3:1–2*

We are not promised to know the outcomes when we begin to follow Christ. We are promised, however, that when we make communion with Christ a priority, we will find contentment in all things.

Love Restored

I'll never forget this day. I received a phone call from a couple asking for counseling. They had come to the end and their marriage was unraveling at the seams. The wife had committed adultery. Unfortunately, this wasn't the first time I had heard a story like theirs.

But there was something different about them. The husband hadn't run away from his wife or from God. Instead, he ran to God, he grabbed his wife, and he called me. The look on their faces as they sat before me was one of transformation.

Yes, there were many tears, but there was also a deeper healing taking place. Something profound and special was happening.

Through the course of our time together, the husband disclosed what God had revealed to him through this difficult season. As he was turning to God and communing with Christ, the Lord showed him that he had not completely given himself to his wife and that he had not been washing her in the water of His Word. This was tragically what he believed had led his wife astray, searching for satisfaction in other places.

This couple chose to stay together and worked hard to do so. They are married and enjoying communion with Christ and with each other today.

In all my years of pastoral work, I have never seen God do such a supernatural work. During one of our meetings, the husband said, "From now on I am going to say to my wife, 'You go to the Lord, and I'll go to the Lord, and we will meet there.'" That is a powerful picture of communion with our spouses and communion with Christ.

The key to having a contented spouse is not waiting for the husband to start loving the wife or for the wife to start submitting to the husband. The key is communion with Christ, regardless of what the other person does. In order to break down the walls of contention, we must be in constant communion together with God. No matter where you are in your marriage relationship today, God's heart is for you to draw closer to Him and closer to one another. There is no limit to what God can do with two hearts committed to communing with Him and finding their contentment in Him.

> If you try to hang on to your life, you will lose it. But if you give up your life for my sake, you will save it.
>
> *Matthew 16:25*

IN OUR SINGLENESS

> But I wish everyone were single, just as I am. Yet each person has a special gift from God, of one kind or another.
>
> *1 Corinthians 7:7*

As I address the topic of singleness, this bears repeating: the marriage union produces the greatest delights and the deepest sorrows. It is the place where many single people believe they will find the most satisfaction and the place where many married people find the most distress.

One of my fondest memories of ministry was the season I spent as the pastor of a group of singles at Calvary Chapel Costa Mesa. During those years, I learned that many singles thought marriage was the answer to all of their problems. In fact, it was very apparent that many of them came to the fellowship for the sole reason of finding a spouse. Praise the Lord! Many of them succeeded, and it was a wonderful blessing to be able to preside over a multitude of marriage ceremonies.

Though some found spouses, several remained single. And within that group, those who remained single were often left with a gnawing sense of emptiness, as though they were missing out on something. There were very few who, like Paul, thought of singleness as a special gift from God. In fact, according to Paul, singleness has advantages over being married.

> I want you to be free from the concerns of this life. An unmarried man can spend his time doing the Lord's work and thinking how to please him. But a married man has to think about his earthly responsibilities and how to please his wife. His interests are divided. In the same way, a woman who is no longer married or has never been married can be devoted to the Lord

and holy in body and in spirit. But a married woman has to think about her earthly responsibilities and how to please her husband. I am saying this for your benefit, not to place restrictions on you. I want you to do whatever will help you serve the Lord best, with as few distractions as possible.

1 Corinthians 7:32–35

Can you hear Paul's heart? Paul saw singleness as a gift because it gave him the advantage of pleasing the Lord only. There was nothing to keep him from being in constant communion with Christ.

Lord, Use My Singleness

Shortly after returning from Israel in 1992, I was sitting in the sanctuary at Calvary Chapel Costa Mesa after the service had ended when a young single man walked up and sat down next to me. I had met him in Israel, and we had become good friends. He shared with me that he felt as though the Holy Spirit was directing him to go to Bible College. I remember sitting there hearing the words come out of his mouth, but it seemed as though the Holy Spirit was speaking directly to me, as though He was whispering in my ear, "I am directing him to the Bible College, and I want you to help send him there."

Here it is, nearly thirty years later, and he is still single and serving the Lord. I recently asked him how he has remained content in his singleness. He shared with me that years earlier, he had prayed, "Lord, if I am to remain single, use my singleness." The Lord honored his prayer. He has completely devoted himself to serving the Lord. He has traveled the world, planting churches and teaching at Bible Colleges in Europe, and he is currently living in the States serving the Lord by investing in the next generation.

There is no doubt that singleness is difficult. There can be times of loneliness. Remember what God said to Adam in the garden of Eden? "It is not good for man to be alone. I will make a helper who is just right for him" (Genesis 2:18). Singles, therefore, not only struggle with loneliness, but also with sexual temptation. So it is vitally important that singles spend time in communion with Christ and with others to help them through the difficult days.

But there is good news! Here is the reality! No Christian is single forever. Always remember that you are the bride of Christ, and one day, He will come for you. You will hear heavenly voices declare:

> "Praise the LORD! For the Lord our God, the Almighty, reigns. Let us be glad and rejoice, and let us give honor to him. For the time has come for the wedding feast of the Lamb, and his bride has prepared herself. She has been given the finest of pure white linen to wear." For the fine linen represents the good deeds of God's holy people.
>
> *Revelation 19:6b–8*

Until that glorious day comes, spend every day in communion with Christ.

A Heart Close to God

> A woman's heart should be so close to God that a man should have to chase Him to find her.
>
> *Author Unknown*

One of my greatest joys in serving as the pastor of a singles ministry was getting to witness God do the miraculous for those whose hearts were set upon Him. My wife and I grew very close to one young woman in our group, and we served together for many years in various ministries. So we were ecstatic when God arranged a miraculous meeting—this godly woman met a godly man. He was chasing Him and found her, and they married in 2017. She described their beautiful story as "loving again and loving for the first time."

During her years of singleness, her contentment was genuine, and we witnessed it firsthand. So what was her secret? She said it was knowing and trusting God's Word. Without a doubt, she was and is a wonderful student of the Word of God.

In a recent conversation, she shared about her life. Early in her Christian walk and at choice points along the way, certain truths based on biblical principles were instilled in her by various pastors and Bible teachers as well as her own study of the Scriptures. It was these truths that gave her a knowledge of who God is—the vast spectrum of His character, as well as His ability to love and provide in strategic and generous ways according to His eternal perfection and faithfulness.

She admitted that there were days she felt lonely and longed for companionship, seasons when she questioned God's timing and wondered if she was doing enough and open enough to meet her future husband. Yet, it was during these times when God's Word kept her anchored in her relationship with Him and contented in her singleness. It was in the waiting, empowered by the Holy Spirit and encouraged by the truth, that her life was given to loving and worshiping the Lord by loving and serving others.

It was this same truth that Paul had in mind when he wrote:

> Now regarding your question about the young women who are not married. I do not have a command from the Lord for them. But the Lord in his mercy has

given me wisdom that can be trusted, and I will share it with you. Because of this present crisis, I think it is best to remain as you are.

1 Corinthians 7:25–26

Whether you are a single man or a single woman, "remain as you are." Be content, for it is a gift from God. Take advantage of your singleness and serve the Lord, just as these two did, and wait and see what miraculous ways the Lord will work.

IN OUR PARENTING

We must seek God's help and do everything we are told to do in order to raise our children well. We need to pray for our children, teach them the Bible, bring them to church, and above all set an example by living for God ourselves.[26]

James Montgomery Boice

God's plan for mankind has always been to use families as the means to govern the world. Starting in the book of Genesis, He gave this command:

So God created human beings in his own image. In the image of God he created them; male and female he created them. Then God blessed them and said, "Be fruitful and multiply. Fill the earth and govern it."

Genesis 1:27–28a

The word *govern* means "to bring under control." God's plan for families is to help bring order into the world, the order He intended. When a family functions the way God designed— with love, leadership, growth, and peace—it becomes a model for the whole world to emulate.

It is important to recognize whose control the world is under in order to understand God's heart for families to govern the earth. First, as Genesis shows, the earth is God's. He gave it to Adam and Eve that they might rule over all His creation and populate the earth. When Adam and Eve ate of the Tree of the Knowledge of Good and Evil, mankind forfeited this right.

> Satan, who is the god of this world, has blinded the minds of those who don't believe.
>
> *2 Corinthians 4:4*

Satan is at work, but God is ultimately in charge. Until Christ returns, the unbelieving world is under the rule of Satan. We are all experiencing the effects of sin.

And yet, it is still God's plan for the family to fill the earth and govern it. As discussed in Part 1, God did not leave mankind alone after the fall. He had a plan, and that plan involved a family. Perfection has never been required.

Throughout the Old Testament, we read of imperfect families, parents and children alike, making a mess of everything. There are stories of murder, rape, and deceit, but redemption was always part of the plan. God used Jacob, a flawed man who cheated his brother out of his birthright, to become the patriarch of the twelve tribes of Israel. God used a prostitute named Rahab to save the spies of Israel and included her in the Messiah's lineage. God used King David, a mighty warrior who slew Goliath but later committed adultery with the wife of one of his mighty men before having him killed, to be part of the family line from which Jesus would be born.

Coming to the New Testament, in the most redemptive story of all time, God used a virgin girl named Mary to be the mother of the Savior of the world. God also used an honorable young man named Joseph to be the earthly father of our Savior, Jesus Christ. Both Mary and Joseph were given the privilege and task of raising Jesus, who came to earth as a baby. Throughout history, God's plan has always been to use families to get His work done.

So you might be wondering how your family can be used to govern the world. God's heart and desire is for the whole world to know Him—His love, mercy, and forgiveness. This is the message and calling He has given to every family who claims and calls upon His name. This is an incredibly noble and difficult task. You may be thinking, *Have you met my kids? Have you seen my family? We are barely keeping it together. How can we spread God's love to others?* If this is you, you're not alone. Jesus said:

> Humanly speaking, it is impossible. But not with God. Everything is possible with God.
>
> *Mark 10:27*

One psalmist wrote:

> Unless the LORD builds a house, the work of the builder is *wasted*. Unless the LORD protects a city, guarding it with sentries *will do no good. It is useless* for you to work so hard from early morning until late at night, anxiously working for food to eat; for God gives rest to his loved ones.
>
> *Psalm 127:1–2, emphasis mine*

The words *wasted, no good,* and *useless* are all the same word in Hebrew, most often translated as "vain" and "vanity." The meaning of these words is "emptiness." Unless the Lord builds your house—unless He holds your family together and guides

111

the upbringing of your children—you will be left with a gnaw-ing sense of emptiness no child or spouse can fulfill. Until the plans you have for your family and home align with God's, you will not be content.

This lack of alignment is present in many families today. While parents love their children immensely, the busyness of life—school, sports, recitals, homework, discipline, and health—have left them overwhelmed and unprioritized. Each parenting book and person gives different approaches to raising children (spanking or no spanking; homeschooling or public or private school; gluten or gluten free), and it's hard to figure out what's right. Our societal move toward two income house-holds provides yet another avenue for decision and potential guilt. Parents have many reasons to feel fear and defeat.

In order for our families to truly be a part of God's plan to govern the world, we must first learn to find contentment within the walls of our home. Contentment always begins with communion with Christ. Once we have communion with Christ, we can have communion with our spouses and with our children. When we prioritize communion with Christ above all else, we can trust God to guide us in the many decisions we must make for our families. God will provide the peace and joy we need to thrive in our homes and in the world for His glory.

One of the keys to finding communion with our children is learning how to see them the way God does. There is a story in the New Testament where the disciples try to make some little children go away, but Jesus wouldn't allow it:

> Let the children come to me. Don't stop them! For the Kingdom of Heaven belongs to those who are like these children.
>
> *Matthew 19:14*

Children are very important to God.

In the book of Mark, Jesus tells the crowds that every person must be like children in order to receive God's kingdom:

> I tell you the truth, anyone who doesn't receive the Kingdom of God like a child will never enter it.
>
> *Mark 10:15*

God loves children. He loves the hearts of children. Many may think a child's faith is the only childlike trait necessary to enter into God's kingdom. While childlike faith is part of what Jesus requires, He may be appealing more so to a child's need for a present, loving parent. Children begin their lives and spend most of their youth entirely dependent on their parents, as they should. This natural dependency is what Jesus desires all people to have for God. We cannot take care of ourselves, just as we can't do enough good works to earn our way into heaven. As children recognize their need for a parent, we ought to recognize our need for God the Father in everything we do. He is the Father, we are His children. There is no limit to His love and care for us.

The book of Colossians tells us that Jesus Himself is holding everything together (1:17). Even the air in our lungs is from Him. Coming to God as His children—adopted and sealed by the Father, Son, and Spirit—is the only way we are able to receive His kingdom.

Recognizing our place in God's family can teach us how God wants us to treat our children. Has God been merciful to you? He wants you to be merciful to your children. Has God encouraged you? He wants you to encourage your children. Has God comforted you? He wants you to comfort your children. Has God directed you on your path? He wants you to direct your children's path. Has God blessed you? He wants you to bless your children too.

Many parents search for parenting manuals to show them how to control their children. There is no man-made manual for bringing children under perfect control. God's relationship with us is the ultimate model for the parent-child relationship. God's Word is the best guide for parenting. Scripture overflows with examples of God speaking to and ministering to His people, His children. God has all the parenting answers; we need only to seek Him and pray.

A vital part of finding communion with your children is recognizing your place as their parent.

God has entrusted these children to you to raise in His ways.

You are to teach them, to instruct them, to love them, and to lead them back to God. That is the essence of your job.

I meet so many parents who feel it is their job to ensure a good marriage or to get their children accepted into the right schools or colleges. They even attempt to control their kids to ensure that they have the kind of life the parents want for them. This simply will not work. These things are out of our control. And while this lack of control may seem scary and cause moments of fear and worry, it is our job as parents to trust the Lord.

In the book of Ephesians, Paul exhorted,

> Fathers, do not provoke your children to anger by the way you treat them. Rather, bring them up with the discipline and instruction that comes from the Lord.
>
> *Ephesians 6:4*

In my experience, children are provoked to anger when their parents are not bringing them up in the discipline and instruction of the Lord. They are provoked to anger when their parents try to control them for selfish purposes rather than for the purposes of God.

What does having communion with our kids look like today, especially in light of the busyness of life? I believe the ancient Jews knew the answer. Jewish men would wear what is called a phylactery on their heads or on their wrists. A phylactery is a little box that contains what is known as the Shema, which states:

> Listen, O Israel! The LORD is our God, the LORD alone. And you must love the LORD your God with all your heart, all your soul, and all your strength. And you must commit yourselves wholeheartedly to these commands that I am giving you today. Repeat them again and again to your children. Talk about them when you are at home and when you are on the road, when you are going to bed and when you are getting up. Tie them to your hands and wear them on your forehead as reminders. Write them on the doorposts of your house and on your gates. The LORD your God will soon bring you into the land he swore to give you when he made a vow to your ancestors Abraham, Isaac, and Jacob. It is a land with large, prosperous cities that you did not build.
>
> *Deuteronomy 6:4–10*

This is what constant communion with Christ and your kids should look like. No matter how busy we are, we must make Christ integral in every aspect.

The good news is we don't have to wear a box on our heads or wrists as a reminder. It already exists in our hearts:

> The only letter of recommendation we need is you yourselves. Your lives are a letter written in our hearts; everyone can read it and recognize our good work among you. Clearly, you are a letter from Christ showing the result of our ministry among you. This "letter" is written not with pen and ink, but with the Spirit of the living God. It is carved not on tablets of stone, but on human hearts. We are confident of all this because of our great trust in God through Christ. It is not that we think we are qualified to do anything on our own. Our qualification comes from God. He has enabled us to be ministers of his new covenant. This is a covenant not of written laws, but of the Spirit. The old written covenant ends in death; but under the new covenant, the Spirit gives life.
>
> *2 Corinthians 3:2–6*

When we as parents find our confidence in the Lord, rather than in ourselves or our efforts, we can safely trust that God will direct our steps as parents and lead us into communion with our children.

Loving When It Hurts

A number of years ago, some friends of mine decided to become foster parents. Knowing that there would eventually be children coming into the home who would need to stay permanently, they decided beforehand to say yes to the children the Lord brought them. After an initial placement of children were reunified with their birth family, a sibling set of three children came to live with them. Over the course of a number of years, I watched as the Lord used this couple to provide love, nurture, and structure. I also saw how their consistency in showing up day in and day out was changing and affecting the children's lives.

One day this couple shared something with me. The comment they most often hear is how grateful the children will be later in life. People will say how wonderful they are to provide for them. While they appreciate the kind sentiments, this is the complete opposite of how they feel. Through the process of loving and caring for these children, this couple has learned obedience to God's will—which, they have discovered, is not always what they would like it to be. When you adopt children, you go through classes to gain the understanding that it will be challenging to love children who have a history of past trauma. Yet somewhere deep inside, you believe that through your valiant efforts, these children will learn to love you, and you will experience the same kind of close relationships that parents have with their birth children. But nothing prepares you for the daily rejection of working with kids with a history of past trauma. Nothing prepares you for the day you realize you are experiencing the secondary trauma from working in close proximity with others who have experienced trauma. Nothing prepares you for the immense strain these challenging relationships will place on your marriage. Nothing prepares you for the day you realize that your dream of a happy family and successful future for your children may never come to pass. The realization of this truth is devastating.

But after the realization that this is impossible, you will hopefully experience humility when you acknowledge you have nothing to offer these kids. *Then* comes the resurrection power of Jesus Christ. Only then can He raise the dead to life.

Getting to share in the fellowship of suffering with Christ through the process of loving these kids, watching the resurrection power of Jesus to raise what was once dead to life, and trusting that God is going to make this situation beautiful in His time, whether or not it ends up the way this couple has hoped, has changed everything.

It has changed the way they experience communion with Christ. It has changed the way they experience communion with one another. It has changed the way they experience communion with their children. And it has changed the way they experience communion with the church.

Over the years, I have been so blessed to see how communion with Christ has not only caused their faith to grow, but mine and many others. Knowing that raising these kids is impossible on their own, they faithfully send out prayer requests. Those privileged to pray often encourage them through the Scriptures. And though not every prayer has been answered the way we would like, we have all gained a powerful perspective of God's will, which fills our hearts with great joy!

The apostle John wrote:

> We proclaim to you the one who existed from the beginning, whom we have heard and seen. We saw him with our own eyes and touched him with our own hands. He is the Word of life. This one who is life itself was revealed to us, and we have seen him. And now we testify and proclaim to you that he is the one who is eternal life. He was with the Father, and then he was revealed to us. We proclaim to you what we ourselves have actually seen and heard so that you may have fellowship with us. And our fellowship is with the Father and with his Son, Jesus Christ. We are writing these things so that you may fully share our joy.

1 John 1:1–4

Loving Enough to Let Go

While my son was still in high school, I coached the surf team of Calvary Chapel High School. Being an avid surfer myself made getting up at the crack of dawn each day easy for me. Five days a week, nine months a year, I would meet the team at the beach. These are, without a doubt, some of my favorite memories.

Spending this much time surfing with the kids, usually around fifty teenage boys and girls, I had many opportunities to get to know them. Although they attended a private Christian school, not all of them came from Christian families. And those who did often were not walking with the Lord. I learned through our conversations that many of them were truly bothered by the hypocrisy they saw in their homes. Their parents were one way in private and another way everywhere else, including church. For some, this duplicity was reason enough to not believe in God. For others, it just created apathy toward God.

There was one kid in particular whom I will never forget. While he was the son of a pastor, it seemed he didn't have a spiritual bone in his body. He was a bit of a loner and a troublemaker. Wherever he was, you knew that trouble was not far behind. Many of the other kids were either put off by him or didn't pay any attention to him. Though he caused a great deal of consternation for me, I cared deeply about him. I'm sure his parents were greatly grieved by their son, but they simply continued to love and pray for him. In some ways, they loved him enough to let him go for a time, much like the story of the prodigal son.

Years later, I was out surfing, and a young man paddled up alongside me. "Hey, Coach," he called out. Much to my surprise, it was this same young man I had coached years before.

He was now married, with children, and was serving as a pastor himself. I couldn't believe it, but his face confirmed that there had been a complete transformation in this young man's life. He was truly a new person.

I share this story in particular because for most Christian parents, this is perhaps their greatest fear—that their children will not follow in their footsteps but will instead reject the life of faith. This scenario is sadly repeated often and leaves parents feeling like failures, wondering, "Did we do everything we could do? Were we loving enough? What did we do wrong?" My encouragement to you is this: your job as a parent is to simply train your child up in the way they should go and live a life in communion with Christ. Even the best-lived lives will not necessarily mean salvation for our children. Here's what King Solomon said:

> Direct your children onto the right path, and when they are older, they will not leave it.
>
> *Proverbs 22:6*

Jesus said,

> For no one can come to me unless the Father who sent me draws them to me, and at the last day I will raise them up. As it is written in the Scriptures, "They will all be taught by God." Everyone who listens to the Father and learns from him comes to me.
>
> *John 6:44–45*

Loving Enough to Be Consistent

> Children born to a young man are like arrows in a warrior's hands. How joyful is the man whose quiver is full of them! He will not be put to shame when he

confronts his accusers at the city gates.

Psalm 127:4–5

Whenever I reflect on this picture, I am reminded of some very dear friends who have been warriors for the Lord for nearly thirty years. Serving as missionaries in Eastern Europe and Asia, my friend and his wife have had four children on foreign fields. Many times, my wife and I have stayed with them in their tiny flat, and we have been so blessed to see firsthand how they have raised their children "like arrows in a warrior's hand."

This terminology may not resonate with us today, but in ancient days, it would make perfect sense. The opposing armies of a besieged city would meet at the city gate. The idea here is that a warrior would raise his children in ways that would enable them to defend him in civil or legal matters so that he would not suffer loss or injury. Godly children carry out justice with honor and love.

My friends are true warriors and wonderful examples of parents who have raised their children in this way. One story really stands out to me. Every evening after dinner, the entire family would meet in the living room. They would begin by singing a song or two, often off-key. Then they would read the Word of God aloud. After reading, they would the discuss the Scriptures. They consistently did this every night, year after year.

I didn't really see the full effect of this until a few years ago. They were back in the States on furlough when my friend and I took his twelve-year-old son camping up in Mammoth. On the drive home, we were talking about politics, foreign policy, theology, and many other grown-up topics when it dawned on me that this twelve-year-old kid was part of the conversation. In fact, he wasn't just part of the conversation, he was adding to it! At one point, he brought up a story from the Old Testament that brought clarity to a certain topic. I turned around and asked him incredulously, "Who are you, and how do you know this stuff?" You could see his father's face beaming with joy.

> It is not by force nor by strength, but by my Spirit, says the LORD of Heaven's Armies.
>
> *Zechariah 4:6*

We put our families in great danger when we try to build our houses on our own. The harder we strive in the flesh, the weaker we become. It is by His Spirit alone that we can build. It is not what we do for God but what He does through us by His mighty power. We must seek God's help and do everything He tells us to do in order to raise our children well. We need to pray for our children, read the Bible to them, and bring them to church. Most importantly, we must be an example to them. And the most effective way parents can be great examples to their children is by living in communion with Christ.

IN OUR CAREERS

> If God calls a man to a work, He will be with him in that work, and he will succeed, no matter what the obstacles. ... Let us then put ourselves in the hands of God and our very weaknesses and infirmities will be used by Him to gain victories that we had never dreamed of.[27]
>
> *D. L. Moody*

For some, work is a place where ideas are created, legacies are born, and money is made. It is the place they feel most successful, most appreciated, and most powerful. For others, it is (as some say) a four-letter word. It's simply a paycheck and a reminder of unfulfilled dreams. Depending on which camp you find yourself in, the tendency for us living in a post-Eden world is to either be overly engaged or completely disengaged at work. In both cases, there is a root cause to our discontentment. Now you may be thinking, *I love my work! That's why I'm so overly engaged there!* I would argue, however, that for most in this situation, there is something more than a love of work driving you day after day. Whether you are overly engaged or completely disengaged, something deeper is driving your discontentment. Remember with me the cause of our discontentment:

> *It is not simply the act of sin (biting into the fruit), but believing the lie.*

> *Either:*

> *God is withholding something from us.*

> *Or:*

> *We know better than God what is good and right for our lives.*

Before the fall, Adam was fully engaged at work. In fact, it was a place where he would go to worship and have communion with the Creator.

> The LORD God took the man and put him in the garden of Eden to work it and to keep it.
>
> *Genesis 2:15 ESV*

In Hebrew, *Eden* means "delight or happy land."[28] Eden was a place of beauty, filled with luscious trees and gardens with rivers flowing through. It had precious onyx stones and gold; animals roamed the land and birds flew in the skies. Adam was put there in this place of delight to live and work each day.

The Hebrew word *work* used in the above verse is *avodah*, which is defined as the service of God, the same word that is often used for worship.

> Then the LORD said to Moses, "Go back to Pharaoh and announce to him, 'This is what the LORD says: Let my people go, so they can worship me.'"
>
> *Exodus 8:1*

So, in reality, God formed man, breathed life into him, and placed him in a happy land so he could worship as he worked hand in hand with the Creator of the heavens and earth. In other words, Adam was totally engaged!

God has created all of us to work, and by work, I don't mean a four-letter word! He created us with a unique ability and mind to work and to enjoy it to produce something useful for Him and for His people.

Often, when we think about work, we think about what pays the bills. But notice that in the beginning God gave Adam work that was both creative and useful. It was a place where he could stand alongside the Lord each and every day, bringing glory to Him in many ways. Your work can bring glory to God! Your work can fulfill desires and dreams and provide for your family and God's kingdom. Yes! It can do all these things and more.

Sadly, many of us are not experiencing this sort of Spirit-filled life in our careers today. According to a Gallup study on the American workplace, approximately "51 percent aren't engaged at work—meaning they feel no real connection to their jobs, and thus they tend to do the bare minimum."[29]

"Another 16 percent are 'actively disengaged'—they resent their jobs, tend to gripe to coworkers, and drag down office morale as a result. These proverbial Debbie Downers are disgruntled about the direction of their companies, feel their needs aren't being met at work and don't fully understand what's expected of them."[30]

Did you catch that? More than half of the American workforce is unengaged at work. They are dissatisfied and are wondering what the purpose of work is. They are certainly not experiencing communion with Christ in their careers. Sad statistics indeed.

We were designed by God for a purpose, for work. Imagine Adam in the garden of Eden, both enjoying and finding immense fulfillment in doing the job that God had given him to do! The fall of man has tainted even the workplace. Don't forget the curse that came as a result of man's sin.

> And to the man he said, "Since you listened to your wife and ate from the tree whose fruit I commanded you not to eat, the ground is cursed because of you. All your life you will struggle to scratch a living from it. It will grow thorns and thistles for you, though you will eat of its grains. By the sweat of your brow will you have food to eat until you return to the ground from which you were made. For you were made from dust, and to dust you will return."
>
> *Genesis 3:17–19*

What we often forget is that Jesus came to set right what once was broken. He came to set free what once was bound up. He came to find that which was lost. He came to restore man back into a right relationship with God—communion. Not worship of career or slavery to work, but worship of God in the fulfillment of man's purpose here on earth. God designed mankind with the purpose of bringing glory to His name through everything that he does: in relationships, in work, in parenting, and in the world at large. You were created with certain gifts and talents to serve Him in your work.

> And the result of God's gracious gift is very different from the result of that one man's sin. For Adam's sin led to condemnation, but God's free gift leads to our being made right with God, even though we are guilty of many sins.
>
> *Romans 5:16*

When our work finds its right place in our hearts and our minds and in relationship to God, our work can be a place of great blessing. In Romans, the apostle Paul told us that God has given each person certain gifts with which to serve Him.

> In his grace, God has given us different gifts for doing certain things well.
>
> *Romans 12:6a*

So often we think the gifts or talents given by God must be used in the church: preaching, teaching, evangelizing, music or worship, service, etc. But God has designed you, your mind, your talents, your strengths, and even your weaknesses in such a way that you can use them in your workplace and bring Him glory. Think about it for a moment. The great businessmen and women that we know today—the inventors, the designers, the creators, the workers, the makers—they have all been given those gifts by God the Father whether they are aware of it or not. The only difference between you and the greats in your field is that your gifts and talents have been redeemed by God for His good purposes.

For we are God's masterpiece. He has created us anew
in Christ Jesus, so we can do the good things he
planned for us long ago.

Ephesians 2:10

I often meet people who have been genuinely touched by
God and want to leave their workplace to serve God full-time
in the ministry. While this is a noble aspiration, I feel that too
often men and women following God feel that serving in the
ministry full-time is somehow more holy or more righteous/
virtuous/honorable than serving God in their careers. This
desire is not bad, by the way. But consider this, God's heart is
for the whole world, that they might know what an awesome,
loving, forgiving, and compassionate God He is through you
and your life. Our jobs are typically the place we spend the
majority of our time and also where we meet the most people.
Is it possible that God wants to use you in your workplace?
Could it be that God delights in your service to Him there? I
think the answer to both questions is a resounding *yes*.

Given that God wants to use us, why are we so often discontent in the workplace? I believe there are two main reasons.
First, our career choice; and second, our employers. So many
have chosen a career simply because it pays the bills. Clearly,
taking care of your family is an important part of deciding
where to work, but I personally believe that God's heart for
your work is so much more than income potential. If God is
your provider, then He certainly doesn't want you to worship at
the altar of the almighty paycheck. He has a place of employ-
ment for you where you can use the gifts He's given you and
be a blessing to those around you, a reflection of God's light.
As to our employers, have you allowed a bad attitude to turn
your workplace into a place of contention rather than a place
of communion?

Consider what Paul wrote to the Ephesians:

> Slaves, obey your earthly masters with deep respect and fear. Serve them sincerely as you would serve Christ. Try to please them all the time, not just when they are watching you. As slaves of Christ, do the will of God with all your heart. Work with enthusiasm, as though you were working for the Lord rather than for people. Remember that the Lord will reward each one of us for the good we do, whether we are slaves or free. Masters, treat your slaves in the same way. Don't threaten them; remember, you both have the same Master in heaven, and he has no favorites.

Ephesians 6:5–9

The word *slave* really jumps off the page, doesn't it? When Paul wrote this letter, it was estimated that one-half of the population of the Roman Empire were slaves, and many of them were Christians. Some were highly educated people who had been captured in the war and brought back as slaves. It was among these slaves that the gospel was preached and received.

There were also masters who were Christians. As they came together to worship, they were taught from the Word of God that there were no slaves but that all were free in Christ. So Sunday mornings, you had the slaves and the masters coming and worshipping together as brother and sisters in Christ. I wonder what it was like on Monday mornings when they all met at work? The slaves and the masters had to be wondering, *Well, what are we to do now? Do we continue in communion with one another as we did yesterday?*

The answer was and is, YES!

The word *earthly* distinguishes masters from the ultimate Master, who is God. Whether your boss is a Christian or a total heathen, you are to obey them "with deep respect and fear. Serve them sincerely as you would serve Christ." Paul was making a point: in the moment we begin to serve our bosses as we would serve Jesus, we will also find communion with Christ within our careers. This is how we put ourselves into the hands of God, and it is when He will use our weaknesses "to gain victories that we had never dreamed of."

Christ Is Your Life

In 1989, I was a sales manager for a packaging company. I was working with five very successful sales people. One of them was a Christian, but the rest of us were unsaved. Though he wasn't the most successful of the five, he was certainly the most special. Every one of his customers and the entire office staff loved and respected him. He was always enthusiastic about his work. If you ever had a question about packaging material, you could call him and he would know just what you needed and why you needed it.

He worked very hard. He started work early every morning and finished late every evening. Your first impression of him would be that work was his life, but once you got to know him, you could see clearly that Christ was his life.

> Since you have been raised to new life with Christ, set your sights on the realities of heaven, where Christ sits in the place of honor at God's right hand. Think about the things of heaven, not the things of earth. For you died to this life, and your real life is hidden with Christ in God. And when Christ, who is your life, is revealed to the whole world, you will share in all his glory.
>
> *Colossians 3:1–4*

An old expression states, "Don't be so heavenly minded that you are of no earthly good." Catchy cliché, isn't it? The only problem is that Paul just declared this expression to be unbiblical. My friend was so heavenly minded that he did more earthly good than most.

I don't ever remember a time where he sat down with me and shared the four spiritual laws. He knew that the workplace was not the place to do that. Instead, he did things like send us all Christian greeting cards *every holiday*. And by every holiday, I don't mean just Christian holidays, such as Christmas and Easter. I mean New Year's Day, Memorial Day, Independence Day, Labor Day, Veteran's Day, Thanksgiving Day, Martin Luther King Jr. Day, President's Day, Father's Day, Mother's Day, and most likely, even Groundhog Day!

Though I was never really interested in hearing about Christ, I don't ever recall being offended by the Christian cards. In fact, I looked forward to getting them. One year, on Father's Day, he gave me a card and enclosed a cassette tape from Focus on the Family. I can remember listening to it and it speaking to me deeply.

A couple of years later, in 1991, he and his wife invited me and my wife to a Friday night movie at Calvary Chapel Costa Mesa. This was not long after I had returned from my vacation in Mexico when we decided to go to church one Sunday a month. It was a Billy Graham movie, and when it ended, Pastor Chuck Smith came out and gave an invitation to receive Jesus. That night changed my life, for it was the night I gave my life to Christ.

Worship While You Work

In 1996, my partner and I, along with two of our sales reps, were invited by one of our customers to a trade show in

Minneapolis, Minnesota, to help them launch a new product line.

There were four of us and four of them. This time, we were the believers and they were not. Near the end of the first day, they invited us to join them for a night of drinking and dancing. We looked at each other, unsure of what to say. Not wanting to offend them in any way, we simply asked if we could let them know later that day.

As the four of us strolled down the aisles of the trade show, one of our sales reps noticed a newspaper headline, which said, "Billy Graham in Minneapolis One Night Only!" He grabbed the paper and the four of us found a place to pray. Afterwards, we went back to the booth and invited them to the crusade. To our surprise, they said yes.

I had never been to a Billy Graham Crusade, but I had watched the movie at Calvary Chapel years before, which gave me confidence. I knew what God could do, so I shared my story with the others. We were excited to see what the Holy Spirit might accomplish.

Without a doubt, it was one of the most stirring/thrilling nights of our lives. As we all sat in the stands with thousands of others, you could feel the Holy Spirit begin to work. A conversation began between my partner and one of our customers. He would ask a question about something Billy had shared, and as he answered him, Billy would say the same thing. It was amazing! Suffice it to say, three of the four gave their lives to the Lord.

> Instead, you must worship Christ as Lord of your life. And if someone asks about your hope as a believer, always be ready to explain it. But do this in a gentle and respectful way.
>
> *1 Peter 3:15–16*

When you begin to worship while you work, the Holy Spirit will move in you and the one to whom you are talking. So remember, true worship is more than an emotional experience. It is the Lord being so present in your life that you give yourself entirely to Him. It is coming to a place where you worship Him when you are alone, when you are at home, when you're with others, and when you're at work. True worship is a continuous state.

Masters Serve Others

> Masters, treat your slaves in the same way. Don't threaten them; remember, you both have the same Master in heaven, and he has no favorites.
>
> *Ephesians 6:9*

Back in 1993, I met a very talented graphic artist who was working out of his one-bedroom apartment. Now, nearly thirty years later, he has one of the most prestigious graphic art companies in the packaging industry.

We connected again in 2015 when another friend of mine was looking for a job. Being that he was a graphic artist, I called my friend to see if his company had any openings. After talking to him for a few minutes, we decided we should meet for lunch and catch up. Our fellowship together was amazing. He began to share with me all that the Lord was doing in his business and how he had stepped out in faith to start a Bible study. In turn, I shared with him what the Lord was doing with me in writing this book. We both sensed that God was opening a door for me to come and teach at his Bible study.

I was so blessed to share that first morning. There were about twenty people sitting around some tables enjoying a feast that my friend had prepared for his employees. Most of them were Christians, but there were a few who were not. My heart was full!

Now, three years later, he and his employees continue to meet together. I believe this is one way we can share communion in our careers.

> You know that the rulers in this world lord it over their people, and officials flaunt their authority over those under them. But among you it will be different. Whoever wants to be a leader among you must be your servant, and whoever wants to be first among you must be the slave of everyone else. For even the Son of Man came not to be served but to serve others and to give his life as a ransom for many.
>
> *Mark 10:42–45*

The Lord Is My Helper

Every Wednesday morning for the past few years, a young man from our church and I walk and pray for our community. He has a radical rags-to-riches story. He was born in El Salvador during a time of civil war. Guerrilla organization soldiers (Farabundo Martí National Liberation Front) would raid homes, killing the males and raping the females. His father took his family and fled to the United States, and they settled in Crenshaw, a city in South Central Los Angeles. Though he grew up in the midst of war, poverty, gangs, and drugs, he knew that the Lord was his helper way before he put his trust in Him.

He married the woman of his dreams, and they have three children, one of whom has special needs. He built a business that ultimately cost them everything they had. He was in a place of great despair, with no one to turn to but the Lord, so he went to Him in prayer. As he was praying, he heard the Lord tell him to take his family and move from South Central Los Angeles to one of the most affluent communities in Southern California, a community known as Newport Coast.

Newport Coast is a very unique area. It is a melting pot of cultures. There are people from all over the world, from countries such as China, Japan, Iran, Iraq, and Afghanistan, to name just a few. Many of these people are millionaires and even billionaires.

When I met this family of five, they were living in a small two-bedroom apartment, barely making ends meet, but the Lord was faithful. In just a matter of three years, he and his wife received an award recognizing them as one of the top one percent elite luxury real estate professionals in the nation.

Due to his success, many of his coworkers ask him his secret. His faithful reply, "All my success comes because of my faith in Jesus Christ, for the Lord is my helper."

The writer of Hebrews teaches us:

> Keep on loving each other as brothers and sisters. Don't forget to show hospitality to strangers, for some who have done this have entertained angels without realizing it! Remember those in prison, as if you were there yourself. Remember also those being mistreated, as if you felt their pain in your own bodies. Give honor to marriage, and remain faithful to one another in marriage. God will surely judge people who are immoral and those who commit adultery. Don't love money; be satisfied with what you have. For God has said, "I will never fail you. I will never abandon you." So we can say with confidence, "The LORD is my helper, so I will have no fear. What can mere people do to me?"
>
> *Hebrews 13:1–6*

The thing I love most about my friends is their faith. It has made them fearless, and their lives reflect it. In a community that is proud of what they own, they say, "We are owners of nothing!" Because God has blessed them with plenty, they faithfully open their home for Bible studies and parties, inviting friends and neighbors to hear from the Word of God, showing wonderful hospitality.

Contentment cannot come from material things; only communion with Christ can provide that. Possessions come and go, but God will never leave you nor forsake you. Man may try to help, but ultimately, he will hurt because he will fail. But if the Lord is your helper, you need not fear. It is when you are in communion with Christ in your career that God will use you to gain undreamed of victories.

Give It to Him

In late 2004, I felt as though the Lord was calling me to start a church in Newport Coast. At that time, I was working full-time as a small business owner and was on staff at Calvary Chapel Costa Mesa teaching a weekly Bible study.

I had started my company in 1989 and had brought on a business partner in 1995. He was also a Christian, and we knew the Lord had brought us together. We had a wonderful arrangement: we would pray each morning and were flexible in allowing the other time for work, family, and serving at our local church.

At first, my partner was behind the idea of my starting a new church plant, that is until business began to decline. We were in different seasons of life; he was ready to retire, and I was ready to serve the Lord full-time. Because of this, for the first time, there was a great deal of friction between us.

We decided we would try to sell the company. We had received a couple of offers, but we both wanted to wait for the right one. As we were waiting, the market also took a turn for the worse. The offers coming in got smaller and smaller, and the contention grew bigger and bigger.

One day as I was driving to work, I was particularly upset. By that point, the conflict at work was unbearable, and the small offers we were receiving left me feeling stuck, hopeless, and frustrated. I wanted out. I began talking out loud to the Lord. In my frustration, it was probably more like yelling. *I started this company! I built it, and now You are allowing all this to happen?!*

In that moment, somewhere deep inside of myself, I heard a still, small voice saying, "Pull over, Jeff." It was the Lord. Reluctantly, I stopped yelling and turned into the back parking lot of a shopping center where I felt like I'd be alone. I turned off the car and waited.

The small voice spoke again, "You started the company? You built the company? I thought it was Mine? *Give it to him*."

It was the first time I had felt the peace of God in months. It washed over me like a flood. God was in control, and I was going to be okay.

Moments later, the reality of what God was asking to me to do set in. Worry, fear, and doubtful thoughts all ran through my mind. How would I provide for my family? What would my wife say? What about retirement? I had a son in college, and I wasn't getting any younger. But I did not give in. The peace and contentment I felt in that moment of communion with God outweighed my fears. I wanted to trust Him with my life, and this test was my opportunity to do so.

I immediately drove to the office and walked into my partner's office. I sat across the desk from him, my heart pounding as I tried to hold tightly to what I knew the Lord was calling me to do. Since he was a fellow believer, I spoke to him in a language I knew he would understand. I simply said, "God told me to give you the company." As I spoke these words, I immediately felt the contention dissipate that had been building between us.

My journey toward contentment was dramatically changed and challenged that day. I am not suggesting that giving away all of your possessions or a company you've built is the way to contentment. But for me, that day marked a moment in my life of total surrender to God's plan and thus began a work of deeper communion with Him. I needed to give everything away, be emptied of self, and filled with Him that He might use my circumstances to bring glory to His Name.

> Or do you not know that your body is the temple of the Holy Spirit who is in you, whom you have from God, and you are not your own? For you were bought at a price; therefore glorify God in your body and in your spirit, which are God's.
>
> *1 Corinthians 6:19–20 NKJV*

Someone once said that contentment is an inner sufficiency that keeps us at peace in spite of outward circumstances. This is the lesson that God wants us to learn—the only true contentment is found in Christ and Christ alone.

THE
CULMINATION OF
THE CONTENTED LIFE

"DEAR BRETHREN, IF WE SHUT OUR EARS TO WHAT JESUS TELLS US, WE SHALL NEVER HAVE POWER IN PRAYER, NOR SHALL WE ENJOY INTIMATE COMMUNION WITH THE WELL-BELOVED."[31]

C. H. SPURGEON

I will never forget the day I began to do the research for this book. I decided that a good place to start would be to see what the world had to say about living the contented life. So I drove to the local Barnes & Noble and headed directly to the self-help section. As I looked down the aisle, my mouth fell open. I felt like a little boy walking into the Library of Congress for the first time. I was so overwhelmed by the number of books, I didn't know where to begin.

Not surprisingly, self-help books bring in about $10 billion per year. Statistics show that people will read self-help books more than any other type of book. With this in mind …

> I hope you will put up with a little more of my foolishness. Please bear with me. For I am jealous for you with the jealousy of God himself. I promised you as a pure bride to one husband—Christ. But I fear that somehow your pure and undivided devotion to Christ will be corrupted, just as Eve was deceived by the cunning ways of the serpent. You happily put up with whatever anyone tells you, even if they preach a different Jesus than the one we preach, or a different kind of Spirit than the one you received, or a different kind of gospel than the one you believed.
>
> *2 Corinthians 11:1–4*

Like Paul, I have a godly jealousy for you, that your pure and undivided devotion would not be corrupted by the "cunning ways of the serpent." Godly jealousy is not wrong because it is an overwhelming desire for another's wellbeing based on love. And I love and care for you enough to warn you about the crafty conduct of Satan. He has been using the same strategies for centuries, and he hasn't needed to change them because they work so effectively! In the beginning, Satan sought to seduce Eve with forbidden fruit. The "serpent" sought to shut her ears to the voice of God, whispering, "Look at the delicious fruit. Bite into it and you will be like God, knowing both good and evil."

Eve lost focus when she listened to the serpent. And we as believers today can lose our focus when we give place to the enemy's lies. He offers us the fruit of self-help and promises satisfaction, but we are left instead with a gnawing sense of emptiness. So many self-help books feed off our desire to be like God, but they will also gloss over our real sources of pain and anguish, telling us in essence, "Don't worry, be happy!" Jesus, on the other hand, offers real answers for real problems; He gets to the heart of the matter, frees us from worry, and provides us with true happiness!

THE TYRANNY OF WORRY

Worry is something that all people do well. One of the Greek words used to define worry is "to be pulled in different directions." Boy, isn't that an accurate definition?!

It is ironic that as humans, worrying seems to be the thing we do best while it is the one thing God desires us not to do at all. That is because worry is the opposite of trust. Worry leads to doubt, and doubt usually leads to fear. Worry causes us to waver back and forth—will we trust God and what His Word says? Or will we go with what we can see and feel right now? Consider what Jesus had to say about worry in Matthew 6:31–33.

So don't worry about these things, saying, "What will we eat? What will we drink? What will we wear?" These things dominate the thoughts of unbelievers, but your heavenly Father already knows all your needs. Seek the Kingdom of God above all else, and live righteously, and he will give you everything you need.

We are so often worried simply because we have not sought the kingdom of God above all else.

The apostle Paul had many reasons to worry. He had been shipwrecked, beaten, wrongfully accused, and had survived an intended murder. Although he had planted a number of churches, by the end of his life, he was locked away in a dark, damp, and disgusting prison cell in Rome facing the possibility of death. I'm sure he was tempted to worry about the churches he had planted and the persecution of Christians happening all over Rome. But when writing to the church of Philippi, he wrote some astounding words:

Don't worry about anything; instead, pray about everything. Tell God what you need, and thank him for all he has done. Then you will experience God's peace, which exceeds anything we can understand. His peace will guard your hearts and minds as you live in Christ Jesus.

Philippians 4:6–7

In a cold, dark prison cell, Paul discovered the key to open the door to communion with Christ is prayer.

THE FREEDOM OF PRAYER

Prayer is the means by which we communicate with God. As believers, we often talk about "the power of prayer" or "a prayer closet" or even "praying in tongues." But quite simply, prayer is talking to God. Most of us talk to ourselves all day long, whether in our head or out loud. Prayer is directing those thoughts, those worries, and those cares toward God. I think that many of us tend to believe that's all prayer is—talking to God or telling Him our thoughts, our wishes, our wants— but that's only part of it. Prayer is also listening to God. It's a conversation.

I love what Oswald Chambers had to say about this subject:

> Prayer is not getting things from God, that is a most initial stage; prayer is getting into perfect communion with God; I tell Him what I know He knows in order that I may get to know it as He does.[32]

The writer of Hebrews captured this truth when he wrote these words,

> While Jesus was on earth, he offered prayers and pleadings, with a loud cry and tears, to the one who could rescue him from death. And God heard his prayers because of his deep reverence for God. Even though Jesus was God's Son, he learned obedience from the things he suffered.
>
> *Hebrews 5:7–8*

The truth is this: God allows difficult circumstances in our lives to give us the opportunity to enter into communion with Him through prayer. Trials cause us to stop and look up. Adversities cause us to turn to Him. This is why Paul encouraged us to rejoice in all things—those hardships in your life, those trials, those difficulties—are opportunities for you to draw close to God, to go deeper with Him, and to commune with Him.

Always be joyful. Never stop praying. Be thankful in all circumstances, for this is God's will for you who belong to Christ Jesus.

1 Thessalonians 5:17

Think about these words for a moment. It is God's will that we never stop praying. When we are having contention with our spouses, never stop praying. When we are having contention with our children, never stop praying. Whatever circumstances we face, never stop praying. The result: we will be joyful and thankful in all circumstances.

Prayer is not only the means to communion with Christ, it is also a source of protection for you.

His peace will *guard your hearts and minds* as you live in Christ Jesus.

Philippians 4:7b, emphasis mine

Do you see the connection? Discontentment (or sin) originates in our hearts and our minds.

It is no surprise that the battle of sin begins in our hearts and our minds, but God promises to protect these two sacred places as we enter into communion with Him through prayer.

A lawyer once asked Jesus, "Teacher, which is the greatest commandment in the law?" (Matthew 22:36 NKJV). Listen to His response:

Jesus replied, "You must love the LORD your God with all your heart, all your soul, and all your mind." This is the first and greatest commandment. A second is equally important: "Love your neighbor as yourself." The entire law and all the demands of the prophets are based on these two commandments.

Matthew 22:37–40

THE CULMINATION OF THE CONTENTED LIFE

Did you see it? How are you to love God? With all your heart, soul, and mind. When we enter into communion with Christ through prayer, our epicenters of worship—our hearts and minds—are covered in protection by Christ Jesus. This allows us to truly love God with all of our hearts, our souls, and our minds, which in turn overflows into our behaviors, our relationships, and yes, even our self-images. Do you want to enter into communion with Christ? Turn to Him in prayer.

THE ONE THING

For the past fourteen years, I have been the pastor of Newport Coast Lighthouse Church. During this time, I have discovered that nothing the world promises will bring fulfillment. Not fame, not success, not power, not wealth. I have learned that no level of economic status or education will ever bring peace and security. There is no religion or philosophy in this world outside of Jesus that will ever bring true contentment. That's because in all other world religions and philosophies, *you* are required to do something. *You* are required to live a good life; *you* are required to sacrifice certain pleasures; *you* are required to make certain journeys; *you* are required to do so many good works.

Jesus is the only one who taught that you can't do *anything*. With man, meaning you, it is impossible to attain heaven. Jesus was so much more than a good teacher or prophet, as so many would like to believe. He was and is the Son of God who left His home in glory to become a man so that you might have a way to spend eternity in heaven with Him.

Jesus is the only way.

> God saved you by his grace when you believed. And you can't take credit for this; it is a gift from God.
>
> *Ephesians 2:8*

He is the only way to experience true contentment: in your work, your marriage, with your children, and in your community. Jesus is peace. He is the way. HE is the contentment which you truly seek. Your journey toward the contented life is *communion with Christ*. The more you commune with Him, the more peace and contentment you will experience in your life.

It seemed the apostle Paul had everything going for him before he became a Christian. In his community, he was *respectable*. He was a Pharisee trained under Gamaliel. He was *credible*. He was a member of the tribe of Benjamin. And he was *powerful*. His "zeal" for God made him one of the most feared men, as he went about persecuting Christians.

But he did not have Jesus.

Reflecting on his conversion from Judaism to a follower of Jesus, Paul said the following:

> Yes, everything else is worthless when compared with the infinite value of knowing Christ Jesus my Lord. For his sake I have discarded everything else, counting it all as garbage, so that I could gain Christ and *become one with him*. I no longer count on my own righteousness through obeying the law; rather, I become righteous through faith in Christ. For God's way of making us right with himself depends on faith. I want to know Christ and experience the mighty power that raised him from the dead.
>
> *Philippians 3:8–10, emphasis mine*

What a wonderful picture of communion with Christ—"become one with Him." This, my friend, is the one thing, the main thing. Knowing Christ, becoming one with Him, is where we experience the contented life—peace, overcoming power, and safety.

I identify a lot with the apostle Paul. Of course, our stories aren't the same, but I see the connections. Paul had a radical conversion. So did I. But when I say radical, I'm not referring to the events surrounding Paul's conversion, which were in their own right truly radical (Acts 9:1–19). I'm referring to Paul's life before meeting Jesus and after meeting Jesus. The differences were astounding. Night and day.

Following his conversion, Paul worked as a tentmaker while sharing the gospel (Acts 18:3). I followed his example, working as a businessman and sharing the gospel when the Lord gave me opportunities. Paul had a specific calling to share the gospel with the Gentiles (Romans 15:18). I believe God has given me a specific calling to share the gospel with His church.

Much like Paul, I've accepted God's will for my life and have left the business world to pursue this calling. However, I don't feel like I have achieved it all or have arrived at the finish line. Paul said this regarding his passion to keep pushing forward:

> I don't mean to say that I have already achieved these things or that I have already reached perfection. But I press on to possess that perfection for which Christ Jesus first possessed me. No, dear brothers and sisters, I have not achieved it, but I focus on this one thing: Forgetting the past and looking forward to what lies ahead, I press on to reach the end of the race and receive the heavenly prize for which God, through Christ Jesus, is calling us.
>
> *Philippians 3:12–14*

Paul was content with Christ, but he was not content with his Christian life. Paul wanted more—more of Christ. He knew one thing—it is only when we are in that place of intimacy that we will truly experience the contented life.

THE MAIN THING

This is the one thing, the main thing.

I love being a pastor. Teaching is my gifting, and shepherding the hearts of others is my calling. There is nothing else I would rather do. But this quest toward the contented life is not easy. The apostle Paul himself was placed in prison and chained to a Roman guard when he wrote much of what we call the New Testament. I have often pictured Paul sitting in the corner of a dark, damp, dingy prison cell with pen and parchment in hand as he focused on one thing, the main thing—communion with Christ.

Jesus Himself often encouraged people to focus on one thing, the main thing. For instance, Jesus was once approached by a man known as the rich young ruler, who asked, "What must I do to inherit eternal life? ... I've obeyed [the] commandments since I was young." Jesus felt genuine love for him and replied "There is still *one thing* you haven't done" (Mark 10:17, 20–21, emphasis mine).

Martha, the sister of Mary, came to Jesus complaining, "Lord, doesn't it seem unfair to you that my sister just sits here while I do all the work? Tell her to come and help me." But the Lord said to her, "My dear Martha, you are worried and upset over all these details! There is only *one thing* worth being concerned about. Mary has discovered it, and it will not be taken away from her" (Luke 10:40–42, emphasis mine).

It is this one thing, the main thing—pursuing Christ above all, becoming one with Him, communing with Him—that will carry us through the more challenging days of life and ministry. When we are able to, like Paul, live our lives according to the truth that Christ has given us, we will find the contented life. This is the life lived for heaven, for Christ, for His glory, that lifts us up above our troubles and fulfills our deepest desires.

My purpose in writing this book was twofold: to give you, the reader, a deeper understanding about the cause of discontentment. But more importantly, it was to provide the cure, which is communion with Christ. You will never find contentment apart from Him.

I believe God also had a purpose for putting this book on my heart: to give you the tools to be set free from a life of discontentment, a life of wandering, and a life of emptiness. God has a plan for you, for your life, for your work, and for your family; and it is a good plan. I pray that you would become one with Him and pursue Christ with all of your heart, soul, and mind.

> That is why we never give up. Though our bodies are dying, our spirits are being renewed every day. For our present troubles are small and won't last very long. Yet they produce for us a glory that vastly outweighs them and will last forever! So we don't look at the troubles we can see now; rather, we fix our gaze on things that cannot be seen. For the things we see now will soon be gone, but the things we cannot see will last forever.
>
> *1 Corinthians 4:16–18*

The one thing I ask of the LORD—the thing I seek most—is to live in the house of the LORD all the days of my life, delighting in the LORD'S perfections and meditating in his temple.

Psalm 27:4

NOTES

1. Dale Carnegie, *How to Win Friends and Influence People* (New York, NY: Pocket Books, 1998).

2. Stacey Colino. 2013. "The Reasons of Our Discontent." *Bethesda Magazine*, November 25. Accessed March 28, 2019. https://bethesdamagazine.com/bethesda-magazine/november-december-2013/why-arent-we-happy/.

3. Ibid.

4. American Fitness Index. 2012. Accessed March 28, 2019. https://www.americanfitnessindex.org/ranking-archives/2012-afi-report/.

5. Stacey Colino. 2013. "The Reasons of Our Discontent."

6. Charles H. Spurgeon, *Spurgeon: New Park Street Pulpit* (Kindle Edition).

7. Stacey Colino. 2013. "The Reasons of Our Discontent."

8. Mary C. Larnia, Ph.D. 2011. "Shame: A Concealed, Contagious, and Dangerous Emotion." *Psychology Today*, April 4. Accessed March 28, 2019. https://www.psychologytoday.com/us/blog/intense-emotions-and-strong-feelings/201104/shame-concealed-contagious-and-dangerous-emotion.

9. Dr. Brené Brown. 2013. "Shame v. Guilt." Brené Brown website, January 14. Accessed March 28, 2019. https://brenebrown.com/blog/2013/01/14/shame-v-guilt/.

10. *Life Application Bible Commentary: John*, Tyndale House Publishers, Inc. (Carol Stream, IL,1993), 301. http://downloads.cbcpa.org/sermons/notes_20090531.pdf.

11. Source unknown.

12. Joseph Carroll, *How to Worship Jesus Christ: Experiencing His Manifest Presence* (Chicago, IL: Moody Publishers, 2013).

13. Oswald Chambers, *My Utmost for His Highest*. Accessed April 10, 2019. https://utmost.org/getting-there-3/.

14. Source unknown. Accessed May 8, 2018. http://www.sermonindex. net/modules/articles/index.php?view=article&aid=33017.

15. Warren Wiersbe, *The Wiersbe Bible Study Series: Leviticus* (Colorado Springs, CO: David Cook, 2015), 206.

16. *The Complete Word Study Dictionary: Old Testament* (Chattanooga, TN: AMG Publishers, 2003).

17. C. S. Lewis, *Mere Christianity* (New York, NY: Harper One, 2015), 122.

18. Ibid.

19. Ibid.

20. G. K. Chesterton, *What's Wrong with the World?* (Scotts Valley, CA: CreateSpace, 2015).

21. *Tyndale Bible Dictionary* (Wheaton, IL: Tyndale House Publishers).

22. Wayne Mack, *Strengthening Your Marriage* (Phillipsburg, NJ: P&R, 1999).

23. Noel Paul Stookey. "Wedding Song (There Is Love)." 1971. Public Domain.

24. Caroline E. Krumm, Mary M. Conner, N. Thompson Hobbs, Don O. Hunter, and Michael W. Miller. 2009. "Mountain lions prey selectively on prion-infected mule deer." The Royal Society Publishing, October 28. Accessed April 10, 2019. https://royalsocietypublishing. org/doi/full/10.1098/rsbl.2009.0742.

25. Warren Wiersbe, *Wiersbe's Expository Outlines on the New Testament* (Colorado Springs, CO: David Cook, 1992), 552.

26. James Montgomery Boice, *An Expositional Commentary, Psalms, Volume 3* (Grand Rapids, MI: Baker Book House, 1998).

27. Anonymous, *Record of Christian Work, Volume 35* (Charleston, SC: Nabu Press), 507.

28. https://www.hebrewversity.com.

29. Gallup, *State of the American Workplace*, February, 2017, accessed August 13, 2018, https://news.gallup.com/poll/181289/majority-em-ployees-not-engaged-despite-gains-2014.aspx.

30. Anna Robaton. 2017. "Why so many Americans hate their jobs." *CBS* website. March 31. Accessed April 10, 2019. https://www.cbsnews.com/news/why-so-many-americans-hate-their-jobs/.

31. Charles H. Spurgeon. "How to Converse with God." *Metropolitan Tabernacle Pulpit Volume 21*. Accessed April 10, 2019. https://www.spurgeon.org/resource-library/sermons/how-to-converse-with-god#flipbook/.

32. Oswald Chambers, *Studies in the Sermon on the Mount* (Shawnee, KS: Gideon House Books, 2016).